MARRIED AND WORKING TOGETHER

HOW WE BUILT OUR COMPANY FROM 2 EMPLOYEES TO 500 EMPLOYEES THEN SOLD THE COMPANY. HOW YOU CAN DO THE SAME.

Michael Gerard Lamia &
Patricia Gallo Lamia

Married and Working Together – How we built our company from 2 employees to 500 employees, then sold the company. How you can do the same.

Copyright 2024 – Michael Gerard Lamia and Patty Gallo Lamia

All Rights reserved. No part of this publication may be reproduced, distributed, or transmitted in any form or by any means, including photocopying, recording, or other electronic or mechanical methods, without the prior written permission of the publisher or the authors.

Although the authors and the publisher have made every effort to ensure that the information in this book was correct at press time, the authors and the publisher do not assume and hereby disclaim any liability to any party for any loss, damage or disruption caused by errors or omissions, whether such errors or omissions result in negligence, accident or any other cause.

Adherence to all applicable laws and regulations, including international, federal, state, and local governing professional licensing, business practices, advertising, and all other aspects of doing business in the US, Canada or any other jurisdiction is the sole responsibility of the reader and consumer.

Neither the authors nor the publishers assume any responsibility or liability whatsoever on behalf of the consumer or reader in this material. Any perceived slight of any individual or organization is purely unintentional.

The resources in this book are provided for informational purposes only and should not be used to replace the specialized training and professional judgement of the reader and consumer.

ISBN: 979-8-35096-082-2

The primary purpose of this book – or playbook, as we would like to refer to it—is to take the reader through the journey that began when we both quit our jobs in early 2000, leading up to the sale of our staffing company in 2020.

We will share the exact methodology that we followed, all the way through building our business, one employee at a time. The reader can expect to personally experience the ups and downs this married couple named Mike and Patty lived through. <u>AVOID THE TEMPTATION TO PERUSE OUR MANUSCRIPT AND DO NOT SKIP A PAGE.</u>

More important, we will identify all of the mistakes we made so you can avoid them. We refer to these bad mistakes throughout the book as **BAD DECISIONS**.

Although our journey lasted for more than twenty years, you can build and sell your business **on your own timeline**, even if the economy isn't doing well or, as in our case, during a once-in-a-century pandemic.

If you have not started your company yet, we hope to provide the reader with the inspiration and ideas needed to start. If you have your company up and running, then it's our goal to help you get to the finish line in a timely manner and experience the big payday!

WWW.MARRIEDANDWORKINGTOGETHER.COM

DEDICATION

To our moms and dads, Jerry and Lucy and Charlie and Olga. Both couples were married for more than fifty years and both now are surely rejoicing in heaven. Their example of hard work as first-generation immigrants inspired us to work even harder and set an example for our children.

To our children, Stephanie and Michael Thomas, both now happily married, educated well beyond our dreams, and running our company daily. They both have exceeded our expectations.

And finally, to Patty, my wife of forty-five years. You supported me as I finished college at night well into my thirties, inspired me to keep reaching higher as I climbed the corporate ladder as an employee seeking a better-paying career, and have been with me every step of the way since we started our first business endeavor in the year 2000.

I am grateful and truly blessed because in addition to being the oldest of three siblings, I was the first one to survive after my mother, Lucy, had six miscarriages.

I love you all.

PREFACE

If you are reading this book, THANK YOU. This is our first playbook, and it has proven equally fun to write and difficult to complete. We did not expect to spend as much time running the company after our sale during COVID-19 in 2020. As a result the review process and this production has taken longer than originally planned.

Few things in our lifetime take twenty years to complete, like building and selling a business. And most of us could never imagine working on any one project for that amount of time before seeing any fruits of our labor. How many times, when you were in your twenties just starting your career, did you think about retirement? Isn't that the only milestone that does take some planning? We can tell you that even though we did accomplish this amazing success, we did not start planning for retirement soon enough. What we read, what we see on television, what we are told over and over going through life is that you start saving for retirement as soon as you start earning a paycheck. But this book is not about that. And we are surely not going to preach to you about that. If you have started saving for retirement, good for you. If you have not, well, there's always time. But enough about that. Let us begin our story.

Here is a fact. ***SELLING A BUSINESS IS HARD.*** That is not true. Selling a business is extremely difficult and given the odds that more than 90 percent of businesses fail in the first five years, selling the 10 percent of businesses that survive after five years is statistically even more unlikely.

In our lifetime most of us have applied for acceptance into a certain high school or college, bought a car, bought a house, thought about quitting our job and starting a business, or may even already own a business. In most cases, all of these activities proved difficult at one point in the process and at the time seemed to be the hardest thing we ever had to do in your life. Most recently we experienced our granddaughters having to apply to pre-K–3 here in Florida. Because of the influx of new residents the acceptance rate was less than 10 percent. This is the new normal. Difficulties are now beginning for young people as soon as they are three years old. But, if you enter this life God has given us with the attitude that you will have to compete to win, good things will happen more frequently than bad things. Our children, Stephanie and Mike, worked their ways through Catholic grade school and high school, earned undergraduate degrees, and then went on to complete postgraduate work. They are now the president and chief operating officer of our company, respectively.

One of the most-recited clichés is that only two things in life are certain, DEATH and TAXES. We can tell you from personal experience that one more activity absolutely needs to be added to that list, SELLING A BUSINESS. It was so hard both times that it compelled us to not just talk about it in social circles but to put our experiences in writing.

In this book we will talk at length about what we did right during our twenty years as business owners, but, more important, what we did wrong. Just imagine that if you already own a business, and we can illustrate ten, twenty, or even thirty decisions to avoid during your time as a business owner how much more quickly you can prepare your business for the sale.

And we will also spend time speaking to those of you who do not own a business but aspire to one day. Image a road map that will take you from step one, identify what your business will look like, to that ultimate step, seeing that wire hit your bank account when you sell it.

Why do you have to get old before you get smart? The good news is that you do not. This book is a real-life story, event by event, of a married couple's experiences. Included are hundreds of examples of what business owners should do in preparation to build a business, then sell it.

Paychecks are okay, but BIG paydays are much better. This book can show you how to get to that BIG PAYDAY faster by avoiding the mistakes of the authors. This is a true story about a married couple's journey. We share our mistakes, then our successes, in that order.

Most nonfiction books will tell you about great ideas, time-saving methods, and ease of getting to the finish line. And some may tell you how to invest the money from your proceeds. Is everyone a fiduciary? This book will do that, but also will point out in detail the consequences of decisions that are not well thought out, the bad outcomes when you do not involve a team before making choices, and the losses you will incur by rushing into decisions. In addition to offering a time lapse of our journey, we will frequently transition into actual occurrences and anecdotal events that turned out badly but could have easily turned out much better.

TABLE OF CONTENTS

DEDICATION VII

PREFACE IX

I. INTRODUCTION 1

II. SOME FAMILY HISTORY, BUT NOT ENOUGH TO BORE YOU 5

III. HOW WE DID IT: BUILT IT THEN SOLD IT 7

    Act One. Where did we acquire the early inspiration? 7

    Act Two. How did we acquire the startup funding? 10

    Act Three. What we did first 12

    Act Four. A year-by-year path to success 16

IV. HOW YOU CAN DO IT: WORKING TOGETHER 83

    Act Five. Your spouse is your greatest partner 83

    Act Six. How we beat adversity 84

    Act Seven. How to identify consultants and con artists 91

V. WHAT WE COULD HAVE DONE DIFFERENTLY 100

    Act Eight. Lifestyle business versus built to sell 100

    Act Nine. We could have sold our first business 103

    Act Ten. We could have built and sold Ardor faster 105

VI. A CASE STUDY: DR. KRIS 108

VII. A CASE STUDY: MS. LOUISE 114

VIII. ON HIRING IN 2025 AND BEYOND 119

IX. MARRIED AND WORKING TOGETHER – THE FINAL CHAPTER ... 124

X. HOW TO STAY CONNECTED 134

ABOUT THE AUTHORS 136

I. INTRODUCTION

On October 13, 2020, the same year the Covid-19 pandemic—the first pandemic to affect our country in exactly 100 years—struck the United States, Mike and Patty sold a part of their twenty-year-old company to a private equity group. Although divesting part of the company was never a consideration, as it turns out, it was a **GOOD DECISION**.[1]

Patty and I continue to draw salary and benefits. We can focus now on the remaining parts of the company we still own and regrow them. This was never the plan, but it proved better than we ever imagined. As a result, our children, who joined our company after completing their college education, now have an opportunity to experience a restart, like our initial endeavor back in 2000. And we have put a nice amount of cash in the bank for our retirement.

---

1   Throughout this book we will identify good decisions too, decisions we think the reader should strongly consider when building their businesses.

FIRM ACQUIRES SCHOOL HEALTHCARE STAFFING BUSINESS FROM ARDOR HEALTH SOLUTIONS

October 16, 2020

The Stepping Stones Group acquired Ardor School Solutions, a healthcare staffing business focused on serving schools. The deal was announced today.

Ardor Schools is a division of Ardor Health Solutions, a healthcare staffing firm based in Coral Springs, Florida.

"We believe that our school division is best served by joining a strategic partner like the Stepping Stones Group with expertise in the school setting; a compelling mission and national resources will support our school employees and help them reach their fullest potential," said Mike Lamia, cofounder and CEO of Ardor Health Solutions.

Headquartered in Chicago, the Stepping Stones Group provides school-based therapeutic and behavioral health services to children, including those with special needs and autism. It has more than five hundred clients and serves 126,000 children annually across 30 states. It is a portfolio company of the private equity firm Five Arrows Capital Partners.

"The acquisition creates additional growth opportunities for us and expands our geographic footprint into new areas including New Mexico and Arizona and enables us to further our mission of transforming the lives of more children, families, and communities," said Tim Murphy, CEO of the Stepping Stones Group.

SOURCE: STAFFING INDUSTRY ANALYSTS

The decision to sell part of the company and completion of the transaction stretched out over thirty months. And never in our wildest dreams did we expect that we would complete the transaction during the COVID-19 pandemic. But we did.

Demanding work pursued us after we sold the first part of the company. Finding support after the sale that was agreed to with a transaction services agreement was a long and hard road.[2] The agreement with the buyers included some of our core sales and administrative staff members. Mike had to put on his work boots and support the company like he did at the beginning, twenty years ago. And he loved it. It is common for business buyers to expect the business owners to remain with the company for a period or be prepared to support the buyers after the transaction, which is what we did.

You do not need an MBA to build and sell a successful business. And with the cost of an undergraduate degree estimated to be $200,000, you may not need to spend the time getting one either. My wife and I both started working straight out of high school. That means we got a four-to-five-year head start on earning money and did not accumulate any debt over that same time. Now, there is a good argument for going to college and meeting your future spouse and other partners who can help you build your business.

I finally earned my bachelor's degree in business when I was in my thirties and did have the opportunity to apply the knowledge I learned in accounting, economics, and marketing

---

2   This is an agreement between the buyer and the seller for the seller to provide post-closing support. The amount of support will vary and can be negotiated. Obviously, the more support the seller is willing to offer, the better the seller will feel about the buyer and the transaction.

courses. Fortunately, I had a 100 percent commitment from my wife, Patty, and she stayed at home late most evenings watching over our two beautiful children, who, as I mentioned earlier, are now a big part of the company's operation. Perhaps I am suggesting that if you must go the route of attending night school while you start and build your business, that is all right! And it would be even better if you had your soulmate there with you every day and night of the week.

We have structured this book so reading it will be enjoyable, perhaps make you laugh aloud on occasion, and as a learning experience. We will illustrate our data in short and long paragraphs and chapters. It allows us as the writers to enhance the reading experience without the boundaries of a traditional format. We hope you enjoy this first publication.

II. SOME FAMILY HISTORY, BUT NOT ENOUGH TO BORE YOU

In this part of the story, we want to tell the readers that, without a strong work ethic, which will carry you through the more challenging times, success may be impossible to accomplish. Both of us were raised by industrious, first-generation immigrant parents. None of our parents had any help from their parents, our grandparents. Unfortunately, for health reasons, none of our grandparents survived long enough for us to really get to know them. On the other hand, we play a very active role in support of our grandchildren, Isabella and Adriana, who are six and four years old at the time of writing.

Here is some history worth noting. Mike earned twenty-five cents every time he swept the four-story apartment building stairs from top to bottom. Patty was eleven years old when she started helping her mom with difficult household chores.

How were Mike's parents able to acquire a four-story apartment building? They borrowed the money from Mike's mom's boss and agreed to pay him back over a five-year period. Anecdotally, that building was acquired in the 1950s for less than $20,000. Twenty years later Mike's parents sold the building for $50,000. In 2023 that same building in Brooklyn, New

York, was valued at more than $10 million. Yes, investing in real estate, like most businesses, does pay over the long run! But that is another story.

As Mike got older, he started working in his dad's upholstery store next to his grade school and, for every day he went in, he was paid one dollar and a fresh donut from Connie's Bakery next door. His career started when he was six and continues today when he is in his sixties!

Coincidentally, Patty's parents, who lived in another part of Brooklyn, paid her twenty-five cents while she was growing up each time she took food to their aunt down the block. Patty referred to it as the rich area because it was a single-family house. A quarter was enough to buy twenty-five individually wrapped Bazooka Joe bubble gums back then, or a pack of cigarettes. Later, in high school, Patty took on a part-time job at an automobile dealership and contributed part of her salary to the household to help pay expenses. She also babysat most weekends. And, like Mike, Patty has not stopped working. She is often in the office fundraising for a local charity.

As you can see, both Mike and Patty started working at an early stage in their lives, and to this day continue to work full-time. <u>One must have an excellent work ethic to build and sell a business.</u>

III. HOW WE DID IT: BUILT IT THEN SOLD IT

ACT ONE. WHERE DID WE ACQUIRE THE EARLY INSPIRATION?

The first and probably the best question you could ask is, how did I know what business to get into? This assumes, of course, that you are not already in business, or that you are considering starting a different one to scale and sell.

Patty and I had different career paths. Although early on she was employed in the insurance industry, her passion for teaching and nurturing led her to a career in a Catholic school as a pre-K teacher. Now one might ask, how could that transition into the skill set that is necessary for starting and running a business? The answer is easy. Although the promise of artificial intelligence (AI) and machine-driven decision-making is on everyone's mind, you still need humans to make things happen. And just the way parents are innately responsible for raising their children, that same skill set is necessary for building a successful company. As we grew over the years and employed more people every year, Patty's skill set became more important.

Mike's career path was very different from Patty's. Like most young boys and men, Mike liked machines. Just after turning twenty and while still early on in his college years, he was able to find a job as a DIBOL programmer in Miami. Almost everyone has encountered the computer language COBOL. It is still widely used as the main language for airline reservation systems in the US and probably the world. Can you recall hearing a printer at the gate where you board? The software behind that program is COBOL, first utilized on IBM computers. Well, the only difference between the two languages is that COBOL was designed for IBM computers, which are still in use worldwide, and DIBOL was designed for digital equipment computers (DECs), which have since gone extinct like the dinosaurs. Mike wrote code, eventually led small teams of other DIBOL programmers, and at the end of 1996 left the industry as a manager of systems development, the modern-day chief technology officer (CTO).

At several of my last places of employment I was forced into using outside assistance hiring programmers. Back then they were referred to as headhunters. Over the years I became friendly with several of the professionals at one agency and became interested in what they were doing to make a living. And it was an incredibly good living—Mercedes-Benz automobiles, nice suits, and elaborate lunches every day. I decided it would be more fun and pay better if I were to recruit programmers like me, instead of continuing to write code as a job.

I can still remember the day I showed up at home early from work. The kids had just gotten home from school. Stephanie was almost fourteen and Mike was eleven. They were not overly surprised to see me home early because when you have a job and you work for someone else, you can get fired. And by the time 1996 came around I had already received pink slips from three separate companies. To this day I am not sure if it was because I was a bad employee or economic situations dictated the employers' actions.[3]

When I walked through the door early that afternoon Patty had that look on her face again. But before she could say anything, I gave her the biggest kiss and proudly announced that I did not get fired, but I was going to quit. In her situation at the Catholic school the work environment was friendly, happy, nourishing—simply different. She would never think of quitting her job because she loved it and everyone there loved her.

In my case it was very different. The demands of my bosses over the years never let up. I felt on occasion that I could never do enough. And I never knew when the door was going to get slammed on me again and I would be out of work again. This new opportunity as a headhunter was performance based. The harder I worked, the more programmers I placed in new positions, the more money I would make for myself, my family, and my employer. What could be better? So, in April 1996, I gave my employer notice and my new career was about to begin. This decision, which was made with Patty's full blessing, turned out to be the decision that would lead us to start our own business eventually.

---

[3] One of the most important things about owning your own business is that you cannot get fired! That was probably the biggest driver that motivated us to start our own business.

ACT TWO. HOW DID WE ACQUIRE THE STARTUP FUNDING?

Certainly, there are more than 100 ways to get the money to start your own business. The most common answer is to seek out family members who are willing to share the risk. That could be anyone in your immediate family, your spouse's family, or even relatives, uncles, and aunts. Of course, that would involve explaining your plan and may even cause you to unintentionally give away a secret that may be worth millions of dollars. Alternatively, you could seek out friends. Do you have childhood friends with whom you share common interests, friends you have known for more than a few years? Can you generate and share a list with your partner? That might be an option. There is the loan option, meaning you now must generate a business plan (not the worst thing to do) and share it with a banker or a third-party lender.

The path we chose made the most sense for us at the time. After work on many occasions, as Patty was preparing dinner and watching over our children, Michael would crank his computer and start writing code. At one point I had several clients paying me twenty-five dollars an hour. I had some experience with third-generation languages, DIBOL and RPG. Both were programming languages that were fading away, but there was still some demand from companies that were having trouble finding qualified help.

It did not take too long to save $10,000. That proved enough money to open a bank account and hire our first computer programmer to go on assignment. At a pay rate of twenty-five dollars an hour we had enough money to make payroll for ten weeks. After the first time sheet was received on a Friday night, Patty was at her computer generating an invoice early that Saturday morning for forty hours at fifty dollars per hour. Yes, that is a 100 percent markup. And the invoice was coded as "DUE UPON RECEIPT." Within a few weeks the invoice was paid and the client was ready to make a second hire. Over the six months that followed our first client hired thirteen programmers. And they paid their invoices within one week.

Next and most important, we started researching banks in the area that would lend money against our accounts receivables (A/R). <u>These loans are referred to as asset-based loans (ABLs)</u>. As our number of contractors grew and the number of invoices we created every week increased, so did our A/R. A key element of the ABL is the percentage of total A/R that we were allowed to borrow against. We found that most lenders were prepared to lend 90 percent of our outstanding A/R. This meant that once we had $100,000 in total outstanding A/R, the bank would grant us a $90,000 credit line. We used this money to fund our weekly payrolls and pay vendors. As we put more contractors to work and our A/R grew, so did our credit line. This was a perfect solution, and it is worth noting that we continue to utilize the ABL to finance our company today.

There are several benefits of using your own money to start a business. You will not have to share your ideas with anyone, except as in our case, your spouse. You will not have to share your profits with anyone except your spouse. And when the time to sell your company finally arrives, <u>you will not have to share those proceeds with anyone but your spouse.</u>

ACT THREE. WHAT WE DID FIRST

We really did start from the kitchen table. The phrase is so overused. One of the largest overhead costs for a business is its rent expense. With that common knowledge, we purposely selected a model home in 2000, the year we moved from Miami to Coral Springs, Florida, with a home office. Inside our new home office in our new home we set up two desks with two computers that we purchased from Brands Mart in Miami. We connected through a hardwire, a fax machine, and a printer. The fax machine was how we were set up to receive time sheets. And of course we had a telephone so Mike could make outbound calls to customers shopping for our services.

Our first company was named HighTechGroup. We established an S-Corporation in the state of Florida and began doing business in the summer of 2000. After Mike left employment at the staffing company, he decided to work directly for two clients, honoring his noncompete. Those two clients through the remainder of the year provided enough income for Mike and Patty to live. It seems like yesterday that Patty would wake up early on Saturday mornings and start processing the time sheets that would then feed our QuickBooks system and generate invoices. We had great relationships with the first two clients and received payment for our invoices almost immediately. We used that money to make payroll the following weeks. It was an extremely exciting time for us. We were working from home and working together for ourselves for the very first time. And in this first year operating our first company, we celebrated being married twenty-one years.

The year went by very quickly and we had visions of expansion. After interviewing a few referrals, including one from our neighbor next door, we hired Chris as a technical recruiter. But we did not want Chris to come to our home every morning and share a 12-x-12-foot home office, so we signed a lease in Boca Raton for a 200-square-foot space.

The excitement increased. New orders for contract computer programmers were coming in because we hired Joe, a former coworker of Mike's. Joe referred Bridget, a friend of his. Now, suddenly it was mid-2001 and five of us occupied our 200 square feet in Boca Raton.

We were cruising along, growing faster than we ever imagined. And little did we know we were on track to bill $1 million in our first full year. Along came Dana, another referral, a neighbor of Patty's brother, Paul. Dana was a top performer for a retail company and had a good presence and a strong personality. She would be perfect for the role of outside salesperson. And it did not take long for Dana to land our largest account.

However, adversity struck our first business just a year and a half after we started operations. It was historical; it would be referred to as 9/11, the date two airplanes hit the Twin Towers in Manhattan on September 11, 2001. Everyone remembers where they were when the news first made it to televisions nationwide. We were all in the office that morning. And, being TV bugs, we had the TV on. We stopped working. We all picked up our cell phones. Patty called Mike Thomas's high school just minutes away from our office. Mike called Stephanie in Orlando, where she was a first-year student at the University of Central Florida. We advised Stephanie to stay in her dorm room until we learned more. We ordered our employees, Chris,

Joe, Bridget, and Dana, to go home. Patty and Mike got in the car and drove straight to Michael's high school to pick him up. The school closed. On the way home we stopped at the ATM and withdrew enough money to live on for a week or two.

The aftermath of September 11 did impact our business. Fortunately, it was already three-quarters through the year and we did reach our *$1 million* sales revenue goal. However, the impact on the financial industry was felt everywhere, even in the small industry we occupied known as information technology (IT) staffing. Our client witnessed projects that were previously in high gear experience slowdowns primarily because of uncertainty. Midway through 2002, because of the slowdown in business, Bridget and her family decided to leave South Florida and relocate north. She was an incredibly good technical recruiter, and we immediately felt the impact of her resignation.[4]

We closed out 2002 on a positive note considering the events of late 2001. We entered 2003 cautiously optimistic about the future. By the time midyear rolled around, Mike and Patty were getting the itch about medical staffing. That itch, that epiphany, or perhaps that inspiration after reading much about temporary healthcare staffing turned out to be life-changing. It gave way to the birth of our second company, MedSourceGroup.

Throughout 2003 HighTechGroup earned enough profit to keep everyone on the payroll and allow us to save some money along the way. But things were not the same. 9/11 took some wind out of our sails; it took away some of Mike and

---

4 Throughout the book we refer to the process of hiring and firing employees and, in this case, the resignations that will happen in the normal course of business. Employers must try to always minimize the loss of good employees. In this case, her resignation was out of our control. We did not look at a macro event such as September 11 as a controllable instance.

Patty's enthusiasm. What was fun for a couple of years suddenly became work. Mike had been in the IT field since 1979, the year Mike and Patty were married. And Patty knew Mike was ready to try something boldly different. And of course, Patty was right there with Mike, ready to jump in with both feet. We were ready to do it again with MedSourceGroup.

Let is take your through a timeline that begins in 2003, when we conceived the idea of starting a medical staffing company, all the way through 2020, when we closed on the sale of our part of our staffing company to a private equity group.

To make the reading easier we bill break it into small bites.

ACT FOUR. A YEAR-BY-YEAR PATH TO SUCCESS

2003

It was early 2003 when we started thinking about transitioning from a temporary IT staffing firm to a medical staffing firm. Although Mike had extensive knowledge as a computer programmer for almost twenty years, which really helped HighTechGroup get up and running quickly, neither Mike nor Patty had any experience at all in the medical field. Patty had delivered two beautiful babies, Stephanie and Mike T., but neither of us had even had surgery before. This startup was going to be different than our first experience, for sure. But that did not stop us from jumping in with both feet. This decision was going to help define us as true entrepreneurs. It was going to take, among other traits, courage, determination, faith, and the willingness to work long hours. The alternative was not very promising. **We would both have to go back to work for someone else.**

We had the startup funds primarily from our efforts at HighTechGroup. Over close to three years, we were frugal, and thankfully so because it was going to take some time before we generated revenue. We also had saved some money along the way, which we did not have to use, fortunately. We were going to need more office space, surely. The 250 square feet six of us were sharing in Boca Raton would not work. And we thought it may be better to move into a space closer to our house in Parkland.

After several months of shopping for space we identified a new building that seemed perfect. It was just about a five-minute drive from our house, maybe a thirty-minute walk, except that it was so hot when it wasn't raining we never walked or rode a bike, which could have been an option.

It was close to the end of 2003 when we started hiring additional back-office support and a few sales staff. We did not spend much time discussing what roles we were going to play in our new company. Mike was going to work with the sales team and oversee the accounting functions, and Patty was going to do everything else.

We are not suggesting in any way that trying to grow a business with just your spouse is a good idea. To grow a business like we did with close to $40 million in sales, you will need help, and lots of it. For this reason, at the end of each yearly summary we will introduce you to the most influential people, who we refer to as key hires, that we hired over fifteen years building Ardor Health Solutions.

KEY HIRE

Faith gave us faith! Patty and I found ourselves in our small, 1,000-square-foot office deciding where to start. Our IT staffing company did not require much in the way of forms. We needed a time sheet so our employees could fax in their hours every Friday. We could then pay them based on the hours and bill the client from the same form.

Our medical staffing business was very different. Our employees needed background checks, drug tests, competency exams, references, and much more. We needed someone who could help us generate forms, so we hired Faith. She had previously worked for a large local medical staffing company. She was looking for a startup opportunity and we were able to give her exactly what she wanted. Years later we estimated that Faith created more than 100 forms. Today, although many of the forms have been updated because of new regulations and changing requirements, we continue to utilize her early work.

KEY HIRE

I knew how to sell. I was successful at my first position in 1996. And my success continued well into the early 2000s. Patty was an expert at back-office creation and execution. She had already raised two children and Stephanie was off to college in the summer of 2000. But we needed additional sales help.

Our second hire, Mikey, came to us from a local staffing company where he had a reputation as a renegade in his approach. He was a young, single guy, a resident of Michigan who wanted to make a statement as a healthcare staffing recruiter. Mikey drove a motorcycle and a Firebird Trans-Am. He sold Kirby vacuums door-to-door in Michigan before he moved to Florida, a skill set we never would have thought helped, but persistence is always an important attribute when someone is selling, especially exclusively by telephone.

He reminded me of myself when I was in my early twenties. Patty and I interviewed Mikey and after a short period of time decided he would become our very first recruiter. It was an exciting time. Mikey was full of energy and enthusiasm and had a promising idea. He proposed that rather than jump into the nurse recruitment area with a bunch of other competitors, we pioneer staffing travel physical therapists. It was 2003, and no other staffing company had made a commitment at that time to try this specialty. Before long, Mikey was on the phone, using the internet and searching for medical facilities that would use our services to help fill their open positions.

Mikey was that first production employee, as we refer to an employee who generates revenue versus an accountant, for example, that does not produce revenue but is responsible for control of the expense side. We provided Mikey a base pay of $40,000 a year and agreed to pay him a dollar per hour as a commission for every hour one of his clinicians billed. In this example, when Mike had ten employees on this payroll, he was earning (1 x 40 x 10), equaling $400 per week. It was a win-win for Mikey, Mike, and Patty. It was late in 2003.

And then came Mikey's recommendation. Mikey had a friend working at his former employer who was also looking to join a startup. Mikey referred Jimmy, and he quickly became our third hire.

KEY HIRE

Although Mikey referred to his friend and coworker Jimmy, he did say with a loud voice that Jimmy was different. Wow, that was an understatement.

An Indiana native, a former union leader, a singer in a rock and roll band, and a very good salesman in the healthcare staffing sector, Jimmy immediately impressed us. Not because, as we learned later, he really could sing in front of a large audience and lead a rock band with meticulous precision, but because he could exert his knowledge and energy and get people to do exactly what he wanted them to do. Jimmy and Mikey in very little time agreed that to grow the business rapidly they would have to tackle the opportunity separately. Mikey would focus on recruiting caregivers to fill the rapidly growing number of jobs Jimmy was bringing into the company. And how did Jimmy bring in as many jobs as he did in as little time as he spent? He sang! He would offer a prospective hiring manager at a skilled nursing company, an SNF, to sing them a song if they would give him orders. He would then follow up with the same hiring manager once Mikey found and submitted a qualified candidate, to sing another song if the manager signed the thirteen-week contract and completed the hire. Jimmy did not complete college. Mike did not complete college. It did not matter. This dynamic duo had something special to offer and we were excited to be part of the experience. And Jimmy's magnetic personality did not stop there. I just watched, and Jimmy led the initiative to build the team, one salesperson at a time.

2004

Then came 2004 and the magic happened—our first temporary placement in April 2004. We negotiated a thirteen-week contract with a hospital in Maryland, which was typical for a duration and still is in many areas. The need was specified as a radiologist and the bill rate was an unbelievable eighty dollars an hour. We had to pinch ourselves. Over the course of the thirteen weeks this one placement would earn our new company $41,600. And that did not include overtime or on-call pay. Next, we sourced a radiologist for the position. That challenge came easy because the recruiter we hired knew someone who wanted the job. We negotiated her pay package and she went to work at forty dollars an hour. The profit that we could use to pay for our overheads was twenty dollars an hour or $20,000 over the course of the thirteen-week contract. And, although we could not count on additional revenue from overtime and on-call pay, she worked both. This was too good to be true, but it was.

We finished out the year with gross sales of $500,000. Six of us were on the payroll, including Mike and Patty, the founders, as we would be referred to in time. At that time, we had two employees helping Patty with credentialing, collecting time sheets, and preparing the weekly billings. Mikey with his two new salespeople made new placements and collected our open receivables.

We did not spend much time contemplating our next moves. The market for temporary medical staff was healthy in 2004. Healthcare facilities, including hospitals and skilled nursing facilities, were willing to pay top dollar for qualified temporary staff. And as the demand for temporary staff increased, the pool of talent increased. Medical professionals we referred to as caregivers were walking away from permanent positions because of the lure of higher pay and the ability to travel to different states. Travelers, as we referred to one group of our caregivers, were in a separate class. In exchange for travel pay and W-2 wages they were and still are willing to accept a thirteen-week assignment in Alaska in the summer months and in Florida in the winter months. Some took an assignment in North Dakota so they could be nearby when a family member had a baby! There were many reasons our travelers wanted to work in any of the fifty states. It was the job of account managers to find those open positions, negotiate the contracts with the facilities, and complete the transactions. I recall one married couple we hired that year who traveled to the same facilities every year completing thirteen-week contracts. Larry and his wife stayed with us for close to five years, completing twenty consecutive contracts over that period. <u>This was not work; this was fun!</u>

When you work for someone else, in other words, you are an employee and you earn W-2 wages—that is considered WORK. However, when you work for yourself as an entrepreneur it is no longer considered work because you love what you are doing, having fun!

KEY HIRE

Jimmy referred us to Ginger. Ginger, like Mikey and Jimmy, did not complete college, and unlike Mikey and Jimmy, Ginger did not have any prior sales experience. All we knew about Ginger was that she participated in massage therapy.

It was not long before Ginger became the third member of the dynamic duo. I guess we could have referred to them as the dynamic trio. Jimmy and Mikey both felt Ginger would do well on the client side of the business, now referred to as B to B. Jimmy asked her to make 100 phone calls a day. He wanted her to dig and find clients that would want to use our services to fill open jobs for therapists. It was at this point in our company's history that we started collecting and filling out jobs for PT, OT, SLP, and their assistants. And Ginger did not stop at calling SNFs only; she started calling in-home healthcare companies as well, digging for their openings. Ginger's reputation as one who could find things buried under a rock stuck with her for many years during her career at Ardor.

KEY HIRE

Our hiring practices were far from perfect, although we were and remain a company that recruits talent for other companies as a specialty. When Patty and I made a bad hire we would beat ourselves up. How could we make mistakes if this was our specialty? Well, as it turns out, we learned quickly that choosing the right person for the job is far from a science. And we were only a few years into building our big company when the light went on. With that in mind, we would continue to make less-than-perfect decisions. Now when we hire a class—more on that later—we hope at least half the hires will make it ninety days. And that is especially noteworthy when a company is hiring sales staff.

Mikey and Jimmy were busy building their respective teams, our teams of the future. Our teams would generate $5 million or someday $10 million in revenue for Ardor Health

Solutions. Ginger was exceeding expectations for John. At that time, she was his only account manager. She was collaborating closely with Jimmy, growing our substantial list of new clients. Mikey, on the other hand, was still going solo. He was doing his best to source as many candidates as possible to fill Jimmy and Ginger's thirteen-week contracts. He needed some help.

Mia was not our fifth hire. But she was number five in a long line of hires who made a huge impact on the company's bottom line. Mia entered the room with enthusiasm. Another new hire without much experience, in this instance as a healthcare recruiter, she had a winning attitude and asked us to give her a shot. This was our first experience going with our GUT on a hire. With Mikey as her immediate supervisor, she jumped on the job boards and started cold recruiting caregivers for our open positions.

We officially had a sales team at that point for the first time in our young company's history. No longer was it just Mikey and Jimmy—it was Mikey's team and Jimmy's team. And what a difference just adding two more to the sales team made. They worked as a foursome, like four tenors or four violinists. We were pleasantly surprised and had no idea what was coming.

Within a year, as Mia was consistently adding to her head count, she asked if we would consider sponsoring H-1B candidates. These caregivers were recent graduates of American universities, mostly Quinnipiac University, which required an employer's sponsorship for usually at least two years to work and eventually become US citizens. That meant we needed to find an immigration attorney to help us, and as quickly as possible.

Whether it was good timing, good luck, or just God's plan, our daughter, Stephanie, was interning for an immigration attorney. Larry was glad to help for a small fee. He had vast experience specifically with matters like time. And our clients were more than willing to bring on foreign therapists with doctor's degrees to fill their needs.

Often I repeat the phrase "the rest was history." Jimmy and Ginger started pitching their clients that had a need for physical therapists. Mia started a recruitment campaign with the university to access as many H-1B candidates as possible.

Like Ginger, Mia had a long tenure with Ardor that lasted until she reached a point more than ten years later when she needed to do something a little less stressful. Patty and I met her socially more than five years after she left Ardor. She was working as an inside consultant for a well-known hospice company. What made Mia a special employee was her ability to be the first recruiter in the company to reach fifty people on her book. At that time, her fifty working therapists, mostly H-1Bs from Quinnipiac, generated $6.5 million a year for Ardor Health Solutions. **<u>The four of us could have grown the company by ourselves, but in our case adding sales staff accelerated our growth beyond expectations</u>**. It had been only a few short years since we put the concept to work, but we appeared to have found the secret sauce.

2005

At the end of 2005 we had much to celebrate. We had almost doubled our revenue, and we invoiced *$900,000* in our first full year of operations. We also made a smart decision we have continued to replicate over the years as we saw fit.

Much of our success could be attributed to the first two sales staff we hired in 2003. Our team of four, each with a remarkably diverse background, came together and created something special. In recognition of their achievements, we decided to give them 10 percent ownership of the company. Previously, we both owned 50 percent of the company stock. After this action we both owned 40 percent of the company and our two new partners both owned *10 percent* of the company stock. It is important to note that at no point in our company's long history did we ever give up a majority ownership stake.

Over the next several years all we did was focus on growth. That meant more office space. Fortunately, the original space we rented in Coral Springs had available adjacent space. Since that opportunity presented itself, we doubled our space, then doubled it again. And the same was true with new hires. Each time an opportunity to hire was given, we seized that opportunity and grew our internal staff. There were some hires along the way that we should not have made. We always tried extremely hard to find the most qualified candidates, but they did not always work out.

KEY HIRE

None of us were the smartest people on the planet. I was the only one working for the company who had completed college. Patty, my spouse for more than twenty-five years, deserved an honorary degree because if it were not for her unselfish commitment to raise our son and daughter while I attended night school in my early thirties, I would not have graduated. But the four of us concluded that to continue this apparent uninterrupted growth, we needed to add to both the recruiting and the account management staff, also known as our sales staff. Let us introduce our sixth most important hire in the company's history.

Mia was energetic, always happy and positive. She helped break the spiraling out of control that happened on any given day when we could not fill an opening because it was filled by a competitor, or a caregiver did not show up because her grandmother passed away, or a client cancelled an assignment ahead of a start date because they filled the role with a permanent employee (yeah, right!).

Now she needed a partner in crime. Let us introduce Trey. And let's say safely that he was colorful. His smiles were always ear to ear, as the saying goes. A Fort Lauderdale native, he had a slight Southern accent, a positive attitude like no other male in the company, and, very important, a desire to make as much money as possible. For the first time in this book, I want to report the obvious. If you are hiring an employee to sell your services, that individual needs to be money motivated. This does not mean we put this desire ahead of our top priorities—God and family—with Ardor, but that motivation absolutely needs to be up there as very important.

Trey had a car that was older than Jimmy's. And Jimmy's car was old, although Jimmy's old car would be replaced by a brand-new Chrysler 300 soon. Trey showed up at his interview with a ten-year-old red pickup truck that had body damage.

For the ten-plus years Trey worked for the company, Trey never replaced that truck. He made a lot of money over the years. He spent most of his money supporting his extended family.

Trey, Ginger, and Jimmy, the leader, quickly became the Dream Team! Under Jimmy's very closely monitored mentorship they challenged each other to create new relationships and put more people to work. The candidate flow with Mikey and Mia providing support was excellent. We were still a young company and one of just a few companies operating in this narrow space placing therapists in temporary positions at SNF and HH facilities.

For the first time we'll introduce our children, Stephanie and Mike T., and the relationship they built with Trey. We are old enough to be Trey's parents, which meant Stephanie and Mike T. were close to the same age and could have been his sister and brother. And they did act very much as siblings who had a great relationship. Stephanie, Trey, and Mike T. loved rap music. We had a music system wired into our office and we did not restrict any music back then. Often when Stephanie was in the office, she would switch the channel and start dancing with Trey. Mia would jump in if she was not on the phone. One of our fondest memories was when one day, Trey gave Stephanie the nickname Webby, after a rap artist at the time. Both Stephanie and Mike T. were still in graduate school, so they did not come into the office every day. But there was a similar memorable moment when Mike T. came into the office wearing a tight T-shirt. It was a normal day, and everyone was going to talk about their business. And then Trey popped up from his cubicle, made eye contact with Mike T., and affectionately gave him the nickname Baby Gap.

As the company, by design, grew and the culture changed, Trey left after a tenure of ten-plus years. We learned years later that Trey joined a startup company that offered him the opportunity to be a leader, a duty and title for which he was qualified.

KEY HIRE

At this point in the company's history, we had more than 100 caregivers, who we also referred to as travelers, working. That put our annual revenue at a target of more than $10 million. Patty and I agreed along with Mikey and Jimmy that administratively we were swamped. Our systems were mostly manual. Jimmy was using three-ring binders to keep track of his business. Mikey was using Excel spreadsheets and sticky notes to keep organized. We needed to hire a sales coordinator to support Mikey and Jimmy's sales efforts.

Our seventh key hire was Jenn. And we did not create a new hiring methodology when we hired her. We were not looking for a college-educated individual who knew everything. We wanted an addition who would continue to build on the spirit of our young company. All Jennifer wanted to do was help anyone she could. She would not be a producer. She would not personally close any transactions. However, she would provide invaluable support to the sales team.

But Jimmy was on the prowl like a lion on an African safari. He had an eye on Jenn from day one. He did not want her to work for Mike and Patty or Mikey as an overall support person. He wanted her solely as his sales support person. Jimmy made his case just like a lawyer in a high-profile trial. His three-ring-binder operation was out of control. Every time his team landed a new client, he started a new binder. We must have ordered more than 100 binders, and they had to be in certain colors. Inside each of the binders were detailed lists of each interaction with the client managers. Every candidate submitted, every interview, every start—no detail was missed. In retrospect, he was modeling a database on paper. He could not manage it himself and manage his team. We gave him Jenn.

Now Jimmy had a team of four, including Ginger, Trey and Jen. He had a team of very important employees. He had several others working for him who did not make the cut. Now Jimmy also had someone who would bring him coffee and lunch. And, what's very interesting about this newest SUPER employee, Jenn, was that she was modest, humble, and did not mind doing anything John asked her to do. We agreed Jennifer's title would be sales assistant. She was more of a personal assistant to John.

Jennifer is still with the company, seventh on the list of our topmost influential hires. Her title is vice president of operations. She is one of the Ardor Health Solutions executive team. We made a great choice when we decided to hire this gift from God.

2006

Our rapid growth became a habit we all became very accustomed to. It was December 2006. We were at the local Hibachi for our first holiday party. The hot sake was flowing. The smiles and cheers were unmistakably original. And as for the four of us—Mike and Patty and our two partners—we were closing the year with <u>$2 million</u> in revenue. We were still a small group with a total of four selling full-time all working closely with Mike. We added another back-office person to help Patty. At this point in our company history, we did not have much of a track record, so we all decided to stay lean and mean. Our leadership team was the same size as our sales force, which allowed us to dedicate much more time to their growth. And we were carefully watching our spending as recognized by our frugal holiday party at a local Japanese steakhouse. <u>We also remained very conscious of our salary expenses. This is a key element to success as a startup.</u> As our business was just over two years old, these decisions turned out to be **GOOD DECISIONS**. And 2007 would prove us 100 percent right!

KEY HIRE

Our eighth hire was our best nonproducing hire in our history dating back to the early 2000s. Our reference to a nonproducing employee is consistent throughout the book. We considered a nonproducing hire/employee someone who was at that time not on the phone, either calling on clients that would give us job openings or potential candidates that we could use to fill those job openings.

As a new family-owned and -operated small business with more than five years but less than ten actively operating, we had been managing our accounting processes haphazardly at best. Although I had completed my accounting courses in college with better-than-average grades, I was far from qualified to provide the support and expertise to take the company to the next level of $25 million in revenue. Prior to hiring Cody, we had a few different people in the role. One had expertise in workman's comp, which later became known as worker's comp. That was extraordinarily helpful because we were actively trying to penetrate more states. Florida, where we were based, was easy. We had NCCI based on Boca Raton right in our backyard.

After we established a playbook for expanding and made sure we had the worker's comp coverage we needed, we needed help establishing adequate payroll compliance in each state that we expanded into. The next hire provided it. We were in a good position to bring on a controller who could bring all the functions together.

Mike and Patty put an advertisement on monster.com, which was the outlet we utilized at the time to source the best local talent. We found Cody's résumé. He was a New Jersey resident who had recently moved to Florida and was working for a temporary agency. He was being paid hourly by his agency, and at the time we spoke he said he could not get away for more than one hour. Now the challenge was how to perform an adequate interview and accommodate his tight schedule. Although I shy away from using the word desperate, like other verbs like hate, we were desperate to fill this new position.

We three—Patty, Mike, and Cody—agreed to meet in a parking lot in Boca, which was close to where Cody worked and near our office in Coral Springs. A few words came to mind as we spoke with Cody: genuine, candid, funny, put together, and, most important, smart. We were impressed enough that we offered Cody a position as controller of Ardor Health Solutions at a generous salary of $40,000 annually. Anecdotally, that position today, depending on your geographical location, will cost an employer between $100,000 and $250,000 annually.

Within one year, Cody championed the move to a new out-sourced payroll system, the move to a new factor that would purchase our A/R at 90 percent, the consolidation of many of our manual processes into automated spreadsheets, the integration with a new back-office product called QuickBooks, and, finally, the start of an integration with a CRM named MedTrak that we still rely on today as our main information system.

As time passed, more quickly than I ever imagined, Cody became Mike's right-hand man and Jenn became Patty's right-hand woman. The four of us worked closely, overcoming hurdles sometimes daily that fast-growing companies encounter. We often worked long hours, but spent time socially enjoying our successes. Jenn and Patty planned ten company cruises before we sold the school division in 2020. Cody and Mike worked closely together, ensuring the cash was available to fund those activities. And Mikey and Jimmy, in the early days followed by succession leadership, set goals and helped the sales team meet those goals.

Cody and his wife, Carmel, became personal friends, which you should approach with caution when you own a business. An old but true expression says, "familiarity breeds contempt." We have had many unfortunate instances of this over the years. But, in this case, our relationship was mostly cordial.

When we divested the school division in 2020, we consolidated our finance division and moved to an outsourced solution. Although I wish Cody's departure had gone smoothly, and it's difficult to separate with long-term employees, we reached a separation agreement and paid Cody fairly for his years of dedication and service.

2007

Little did we know entering this new year that it was going to be a big one. The number of job orders we could fill continued to increase. It appeared on occasion that we were the only medical staffing company focusing on therapy. We grew to more than 100 travelers on assignment. We needed to start thinking about more space.

Mike arranged a meeting with the landlord, Billy. He was a Southern guy who always wore a warm smile and greeted me with an equally warm handshake. And the relationship we had with Billy was a big reason we were able to continually hire more sales staff. Billy never said no. And this time Billy had a great opportunity, probably the best we could have wished for. A real estate company had just vacated half the third floor. At that time, we were on the second floor, occupying about one half of the space.

We moved into our first real office, Class A, elevators, outdoor signage, after about two and a half years of operation. It was exciting but scary. The rent was tripling. How could we pay it without increasing our sales? But that pressure worked in our favor. I remember the office. We had five separate offices, each with room for five desks. We financed enough desks for the ten of us to fill two rooms. The other three rooms were empty. **GOOD DECISION**.

The year 2007 was going to be our breakout year as a new startup. And there would be many more to follow. We increased our revenue two and a half times. We were now a _$5 million_ company. We were in a new space never rented before with fresh paint and bright lights shining through the clean windows. And the space even had a kitchen so we could all eat lunch at our desks. Every one of us was driven by the same motivation. We wanted to succeed, make money, and have as much fun as possible.

KEY HIRE

As you and your spouse or partner are growing your company for a potential sale, you can never know which employee will have an impact, if any, on the long-term growth of your operation. Admittedly, and statistically, most of the applicants you hire—and each of them at the time seem perfect and too good to be true—will not last. We were in and continue to be in the business of evaluating humans. We are a staffing company. We evaluate talent for our outside clients, and we evaluate talent for internal hires to support our external clients. We never hired someone we did not like. It would be fantastic for us to hit the mark 100 percent of the time. Unfortunately, that's not reality.

In the instance of our ninth hire, a real all-star, we met and hired Shervin as a consultant. Companies with a vision of $25 million in sales need a few very important components: a highly qualified accounting department, which Cody spearheaded, and an equally strong technology initiative, which Shervin spearheaded.

Mike was able to use Microsoft Access and Microsoft Excel to build a database suitable for a $10 million company. But that solution would not be suitable for a company that wanted to grow to $25 million or more. Shervin was referred by Mikey and Jimmy. Shervin, we learned later, performed consulting services for Mikey's and Jimmy's prior employer. Shervin had something extremely important in his background. He wrote code for another medical staffing company. Voilà, whether it was luck, fate, or God's plan, we found a component we needed, a component that was invaluable.

Hiring Mr. Humility felt more like destiny. He was and still is a local Boca Raton resident and a fantastic listener, which is important as an information system is built out. He solely and independently built out a system integrated with every part of our business. He took my mix of spreadsheets, Word documents, and napkin-based templates and turned it into a working system for close to fifty users in less than twenty-four months. And not only was Shervin an excellent software developer, but his cultural fit was also unprecedented. He was right there on the dance floor at every holiday party. He spoke with confidence and assurance at every quarterly meeting, always positive about the direction we were taking. He attended both Stephanie's wedding in Ashville and Mike T.'s wedding in Tampa. He, like Cody and Jenn and so many others, became a member of the family business.

As our first book goes into production in 2024, Shervin has launched a version of MedTrak that we plan to offer as a subscription to other healthcare staffing companies based in the United States. Our ninth employee, still a current partner, was special, and we are thankful we found him.

KEY HIRE

Special people come into our lives unexpectedly. When Mike and Patty interviewed Brooke, something about her was special. Her smile was distinctive. Was she going to be that next hire who would set the tone for a new class of Ardor Health recruiters? She left Mike's office after the interview and said she would have to think about the opportunity. She said she would call her husband from the car and ask him what he thought. I remembered a saying our pastor used when he was asking for contributions: that if you did not give graciously, you would benefit from misfortunes. With a sincere and most serious look, I said that to Brooke before she left the interview. It worked!

Brooke was a graduate of Florida State University. Her dad was chief of police in Virginia Beach. She was our first hire from a different generation, a different breed. Soon after Brooke was hired, she became a friend of Stephanie's. They were about the same age. Stephanie was still in law school at Saint Thomas University in Miami, so most of their time was spent together on the weekend. Although Brooke was already married and Stephanie had been dating Manny for many years, they shared a common bond. Neither was happy in their relationship. But Ms. Patty was there to assist. The three of them often met for lunch and talked. Patty had adopted a second daughter in Brooke. And we included Brooke in most of our family events. I recall one instance when we were invited to a preview of NetJet's newest models at the Fort Lauderdale executive airport. The girls were all dressed up, looking better than most. Being the conservative, I was inside the smallest jet looking at the configuration.

Suddenly, Patty and I heard Brooke across the hangar shouting, "Daddy, I want the big one!" She did become one of the family in our family business.

There were far too many hires between the first and the tenth special hires who did not make the cut. But our first ten special hires were a big part of the reason for our long-term success. As we approached our fifth year of operations, we knew that most small companies had already failed by now. But our ten special hires to date were all still with us, working as a team and, as important, as a family and giving every ounce of effort to guarantee our success.

It is noteworthy where these ten special employees are now in 2024. As owners, operators, shareholders, and family members, we must expect life changes, and although we as employers do our best to retain the talent we hired with the greatest expectations, we will lose some of that talent.

Brooke was our second healthcare staffing recruiter to reach fifty travelers working. At this point in the company's history, the weekly billing for each traveler approximated $2,500. At her peak, Brooke was generating $125,000 in weekly billing for the company. Annualized that was over $6 million. Would you like to ensure that employee is happy?

The story ended well. Brooke reconnected with a high school sweetheart in Virginia Beach. They were to be married. When she approached Patty and me with Stephanie by her side, all we could do was wish her well and offer any support she needed, for as long as she needed it. As a superstar person and recruiter, she immediately found a new position as an internal recruiter for a large hospital in Virginia. She is now a mother of two beautiful children. To this day, we remain in touch with Brooke and her family.

2008

After a fun-filled 2007 with *$5 million* and sales, and a profit margin of 10 percent at the bottom line, the four of us decided in quick fashion it was time to expand again. We had the space to hire at least ten more employees. We had enough cash flow to support the additional salaries. We bought and built ten more chairs purchased from our local Costco. We set up a business account with Dell and negotiated twelve months' free interest on our purchases. We were ready to do it again!

Mike and Patty set up an account on Monster.com and posted a position for healthcare recruiters. As we shifted our daily routines toward reviewing résumés, performing interviews, and making job offers, our two partners along with the small but motivated sales staff kept on selling. Now that we were close to reaching the five-year mark as a startup company, our confidence was growing, and we were willing to take more risks.

KEY HIRE

The success of a startup really does rely on the success of the people hired. At this point in our company's history, nine of our first ten special employees were all still working for the company. Mikey and Jimmy, our first two hires, were still leading the sales team. Mia and Brooke emerged as a great tandem and were filling jobs opened by Ginger and Trey. Jenn was the glue that held together the sales team. There were internal feuds that are normal. But Jenn was there as a referee all day and every day. Cody emerged as a controller. He sourced multiple opportunities for options in payroll and HR processing and payroll funding and became our default chief of humor.

Shervin quietly built out a robust database that interconnected every department within the company. We were having fun, growing the company, and ready to resume our hiring pattern.

Number eleven on our special twenty-five list emerged from a very different background and personality. As a new startup operating in an area of the county where many of the largest healthcare staffing companies operated, we had to be respectful of applicants currently employed by our competitors, especially the larger and publicly traded companies that had deep pockets, if an allegation of a broken noncompete was filed.

We never considered an applicant who may bring a problem along with a hire, except in this first instance when we interviewed and hired Sadie. She had a great attitude. She had something in her background no other recruiter had: relevant experience. When she left the publicly traded company across town to join our startup, she had fifty travelers in her book and an assistant.

Not long after Sadie started working for Mikey and joined the team with Mia and Brooke, she asked us for a meeting. In that meeting, Sadie boldly stated she could personally, without any sales assistance, get fifty people working within one year. No one so far was able to achieve that feat in one year. She then proceeded to ask us what we would do for her if she reached her goal. Patty and I, puzzled at her request, looked at each other, and I responded by telling her we would give her a $5,000 bonus if she hit the goal. Well, this hard-working, self-starting mother of two hit the goal in six months.

At that moment in the company's young history I for the first time equated the desire to succeed with the need to feed the family. Sadie was the first salesperson we hired and was married with children. She had an interest in succeeding that was greater than that of any other employee we had ever hired. And Sadie had one additional skill that would be new to our team. Although she was hired as a recruiter, not as a part of the leadership team like Mikey and Jimmy, she had leadership abilities. Mia and Brooke, it seemed naturally, started following her lead.

2009

The great run continued throughout 2008 as we closed out the year with *$9 million* in sales while maintaining a 10 percent profit to the bottom line. Our investments in infrastructure and personnel were paying dividends. We had increased our top line sales the year before by 250 percent. In 2008 we increased our top line sales by close to 100 percent. It was time to look at our infrastructure and ensure we had adequate support in place to sustain our incredible growth. We were using a desktop version of QuickBooks, a similar system to what Costco uses. But that system was limited to a single user. QuickBooks offered an enterprise version that was web based and supported multiple users. With these additional capabilities we could have multiple employees logged on to perform different tasks such as entering payrolls, processing accounts payables, and posting cash through their A/R module. The decision was an easy one, and we executed the transition in one week. Staying nimble is always a great strategy. We did not need multiple meetings to come to this decision.

We also had to look at our information system. We employed a part-time contractor for support, but it was time to bring Shervin on full-time. Adding more capabilities to our MedTrak homegrown system would help ensure we continued to grow at the pace we had become used to. For our $10 million-plus company, the decision to build versus buy and information system was a **GOOD DECISION**. With these two decisions we now had an added comfort level and paved the way for the company to grow to $25 million in sales.

But something else, something special, something unique, was happening in 2009. Although there was a financial crisis, the first one in many years, our business was sustaining its growth path. And for that reason, we were contacted by an M&A specialist named Jack. He was a special kind of guy with a very heavy Boston accent. That was one of the reasons we were attracted to Jack, along with his suggestion that our company may be worth a lot of money if we were to take it to market.

We met Jack in person one summer afternoon in Chicago while attending the Staffing Industry Analysts annual event. We had already spoken on the telephone several times, but this was going to be the first time we met Jack face-to-face. Patty and I were quite surprised when we heard Jack's voice as he called out to us in the large hall. His outfit did not match his strong Boston accent. Jack was wearing blue jean shorts, white socks, and sneakers. Was this going to be the guy to represent our company in a sale process? Well, as the old saying goes, "don't judge a book by its cover."

What happened over the next several months was an incredible learning experience. Jack showed us and our two partners in detail how to develop our book, the book necessary to share our story with prospective buyers. Jack then shared a copy of his database that contained close to 1,000 prospective buyers of healthcare staffing companies. Jack coached me how to speak with prospective buyers who showed interest in acquiring our company. Jack reminded us repeatedly that we had a healthy physical therapy (PT) company worth a lot of money. This experience was unique and exciting, and we were starting to imagine what millions of dollars in cash might look like in our joint checking accounts.

As the process continued, several months in, we were contacted by a private equity company that was especially interested in acquiring our business. Everything was going great and the possibility of a deal closing and us cashing out was looking stronger than ever until one afternoon at our Coral Springs office, we were told the private equity group was concerned about the slowing economy and was backing out of the transaction. Our hearts sank; we were so close to selling our company for $10 million only five years after we started it. This is when we made a **BAD DECISION**. Rather than wait out the bad economy which came back less than twelve months later, we took the company off the market. **We were growing like wildfire and that was the best time to try and sell.**

KEY HIRE

Job orders were plentiful. Our small team of account managers was working long hours and expanding its client base. At that time, we had hired and terminated several account managers along the way. Most were able to achieve early success, what is known as gathering the low-hanging fruit. But as the effort to grow from a fast start faded, we watched several leave the organization. Fortunately for the account managers who succeed, they would be given the accounts for further nurturing. And our job order count just kept growing.

The four of us in leadership decided we should hire more recruiters. In our industry, it was common to have two or more recruiters for every account manager. Recruiting and retaining caregivers every thirteen weeks proved much more difficult than seeking and keeping new accounts. Candidates were in high demand.

We recruited and hired Lana. She had some industry experience where she was in a supervisory role. We were forward-thinking at that time, recognizing that at some point we would need to grow our leadership team. She was closer in personality to Sadie, more serious. But she was a producer. And like our experience of hiring account managers who would not stay employed with Ardor Heath very long, we hired and eventually terminated several recruiters along the way. Having Sadie and now Lana in light supervisory roles helped us grow. Lana and Sadie had a few attributes in common. They both were older, they both had families they were supporting, and they would both end up in senior leadership roles at some point in their employment with the company.

KEY HIRE

We were not planning to add to our team of account managers until we received a résumé from a candidate who had just relocated to Coral Springs from the Orlando area. During that period in our company's history, we would not have considered a remote employee. When a qualified candidate moved into our geographic area, we knew we needed to move fast. And Rob was qualified. He had spent the previous two years working for the largest privately held medical staffing company in the country. We were and continue to be very conscious of candidates applying for work who have noncompete agreements with their current employers. We always ask to review such agreements before making an offer of employment. Rob's was typical. He could not work for a competing firm within fifty miles of his current company's location. We were good!

Rob was single and had a college degree. He was only our second hire, along with Brooke, who had completed college. We preferred college degrees, but we did not make them mandatory.

Rob's degree was from the same university our son and daughter graduated from, the University of Central Florida. This was a good connection. We were ready to add Rob to the family.

Rob had to start at the bottom, dialing the telephone and gaining new clients where we could place our caregivers. He fit in well with the team and quickly became a lead account manager. Before he left the organization late in 2016 to start his own company, he was promoted all the way to the top, third in line under Mike and Patty.

2010

Our blockbuster growth seemed to be without resistance when we recorded another record sales year of *$14 million* in 2009. Our back-office support saw continued growth. We now had very qualified individuals in accounting performing weekly payroll, weekly payables processing, and daily cash posting. Similarly, in our quality assurance department, we doubled our staff. Every time we locked in a new traveler we had to verify their background and ensure they could pass competency tests in the areas of expertise. Additionally, we always performed reference checks by telephone to ensure our therapists were meeting the expectations of our clients. All these tasks were performed by our quality assurance department.

We also formalized the reporting structure for the first time. Every employee in the company reported to someone in a supervisory capacity. This created a form of redundancy throughout the organization. If an employee left without notice, we would be able to continue without much interruption. And finally, the sales organization, composed of recruiters and account managers, needed to continue to grow. We had plans to place our caregivers in all fifty states. That would require at least ten account managers assigned to individual states. Our goal was to hire twenty recruiters to support those account managers. We were well on our way to meeting both goals by the end of 2010.

The four of us agreed it was time for a celebration. Each year as we set and exceeded goals we rewarded the staff. This year we decided to reward the staff with company-paid cruises that included spouses. We left our offices on a bus, Friday late in the day, and returned to the office on Monday late morning, where we enjoyed pizza and reflected on the weekend. The entire time the staff stayed connected and busy. On this special occasion, one of the members of our leadership team was found naked face down in his room. He did not mean harm to anyone; he just drank too much!

On a different day, my wife and I were walking around the ship when we passed by a bar with a lot of noise coming from inside. We found another member of our leadership team with a microphone rapping with 100 other guests. One final memory involved yet another member of the management team. After breakfast one morning, we saw him with a bandage covering his nose. It appeared he had been hit. He did in fact tell us that at karaoke the night before he had told someone he could not sing. The performer subsequently punched him in the nose. We were all breathless after hearing the story. Well, as it turned out, yet another one of our managers drank too much and hit his nose getting out of the shower! Over the next ten years, we cruised every year. And each one of those trips rewarded us with permanent memories and higher subsequent sales. **Good decision**.

KEY HIRE

Again, we felt we had enough talent at the account manager level and we needed to hire at least two or three more very qualified recruiters. We had had very good experience sourcing candidates with good or very good experience in our industry. But you never know where your next superstar will emerge from. From a bank?

Rita had a great interview. She would break the mold if we followed through with her hire. She was to be the oldest recruiter we ever hired. She was a Midwest native with a fantastic personality. She was at a point in her life where she was looking for a career change. She had so much in common with Patty; they were the same age. She was, however, single with an adult son. She wanted to make as much money as possible as she entered this new era in her career. With her smile that always made others smile, she grew her book of business as fast as Sadie did. She reached the pinnacle of fifty working caregivers before she reached year two.

Rita stayed with us through thick and thin. She witnessed four leadership changes before she agreed to join the Stepping Stones Group in late 2020 after we diversified our school division. Patty continues to be friends with Rita on Facebook. She was dedicated; she is still working as a recruiter for SSG.

KEY HIRE

We were continuing our record growth and we needed more recruiters. At this point we were continually posting advertisements on LinkedIn for medical recruiters. Mikey had to hire someone to help with the recruiting effort. The résumés were coming in fast and furiously. We were about to witness another first. We hired Rhonda. If we were not surprised enough that we hired a former banker with no experience who would become a top recruiter, then we hired someone from Victoria's Secret. She had absolutely no experience in our industry but had one very common trait. She wanted to make a lot of money, and she wanted to do it as fast as possible. Recognizing this desire when hiring staff for a production role is critical. A college degree is nice. Having specific industry experience, especially from a competing firm, is even better, but the desire to succeed rates the highest. And Rhonda had a more serious way about her. For these reasons, she also increased her book of business to fifty rapidly.

Rhonda became a wife and a new mom very recently. After a very long, successful career with Ardor Health Solutions, Rhonda left the company after more than ten years.

2011

I finished my high school years in Miami, Florida, at Palmetto Senior High. During my junior year my dad bought me my first car, a 1966 Ford Mustang. She was baby blue and although she only had a six-cylinder engine and an automatic transmission, I could spin the rear wheels when I wanted to. She only had AM/FM radio, which meant I had to make an investment in new technology so I could listen to my music. That new technology was an eight-track tape deck. And I bought the carrying case so I could take it in and out of the car. The case held ten eight-track tapes. And at a time when rock and roll was most popular, most of my tapes were Aerosmith. "The train kept a rolling all night long." I played that song over and over. Maybe that was part of my destiny.

The year 2010 marked the beginning of a new decade. It had already been ten years since the threat of Y2K hung over all of the power grids in the United States. That did not happen. But what did happen was our startup company, known as Ardor Health Solutions, crossed the *$20 million* sales mark. In just six short years but with a lot of long days and unending focus, we went from $0 to $20 million. And we celebrated, in a generous and extraordinary way, and invited the entire staff and their spouses on a weekend cruise out of Port Everglades. Patty and I also made an especially important decision to reward Mikey and Jimmy our close business partners. Mike and Patty now owned 52 percent, a majority, and Mikey and Jimmy both owned 24 percent each of the company stock. Our entire team was motivated to continue our growth into the next decade.

KEY HIRE

A young and very quiet lady joined our company almost fifteen years ago. Lourdes was interested in joining a startup company in Coral Springs rather than continuing to work for a much larger company run by a private equity group. She was another in a series of good hires who had relevant experience, was a good communicator, and was eager to demonstrate her experience. She hit it off with Patty at the first interview and their relationship has grown every year since. We were in desperate need of additional resources in our growing quality credentialing department. At this point in time, we were expecting each member of that department to support up to fifty travelers. The team felt Lourdes was up to the job.

Lourdes's family was from Orlando. She worked in the Boca Raton, Coral Springs area because that was where she could find work. She missed being home with her family. So even before the COVID-19 pandemic closed our offices in Coral Springs, we willingly accepted her request to work remotely and move back to Orlando.

To this day, Lourdes is still employed and is one of the hardest-working team members we have working in our credentialing department. Our company would not have grown as quickly without Lourdes's dedication. We are very proud of her and are greatly appreciative of her every day. Lourdes remains one of our top-quality control leaders and a very key employee.

2012

We entered the new year excited about our prospects for continued growth. The year 2011 had been another record-breaking year with *$25 million* in sales. Our team was peaking, but not everything was smelling rosy for the first time at Ardor Health Solutions. As individuals reached new highs, personalities started to exert new traits that were not necessarily good for the overall health of the organization. Mikey and Jimmy were now approaching their ten-year anniversary with the company. They both owned 24 percent of the company, or collectively almost half of all the outstanding stock.

At this point in our company's history, Mike and Patty were titled senior vice president and Mikey and Jimmy were titled vice president. We did not appoint a CEO as, at least in my opinion, we did not need that formal structure in our mid-sized company. And the relationship Mikey and Jimmy had had well before they joined us in 2004 seemed to be dwindling. There were differing opinions about the direction the company should take, at least from a sales perspective. Jimmy was seeking more power. Mikey was resisting Jimmy's advances. A battle we had never anticipated was brewing.

This distraction was also affecting the sales effort. We were seeing fewer transactions on a weekly basis. We were used to closing thirty transactions every week. Net cancellations by our clients and our caregivers, which were very normal at that time, we were netting twenty-five transactions a week. Considering that our average contracts were thirteen weeks in length, we were tracking toward 325 contingent workers in the field, a level we had never reached in prior years. But the apple cart was getting upset. Unrest was starting to spread as our two sales leaders were not the dynamic duo the sales force was used to working for.

Patty and I were forced into making a tough decision, one we never planned for, had no experience with, and were uncomfortable moving forward with. We had to figure out a way to move Jimmy out of the forefront. Mikey was more than capable of running the entire sales force that now was close to twenty-five in number.

We met with Jimmy and offered him a different position in the organization. With the blessing of our corporate attorney, we also made Jimmy aware that if he did not accept the new position, it would impact his weekly pay. We were not surprised when Jimmy was extremely disappointed in our offer and chose to negotiate a mutual termination from the company. Because Jimmy owned 24 percent of the company stock he was in line for a generous payout over a three-year period. It was at this time that Patty and I first accepted the fact that giving Jimmy so much equity in the company was not the best idea. But in the end it all worked out. Jimmy eventually left South Florida and relocated to Las Vegas, where he always spoke about going after Ardor.

KEY HIRE

Around the same time, we were continuing to recruit and add to our account management team. Patty remained a key member of the team, responsible for interviewing everyone who was applying for positions throughout the company. One morning a shy, young man named Franky was introduced. Most notably he was also from Orlando and working for a small medical staffing company. He was interested in relocating to

South Florida in order to be close to the beach. Patty admittedly was not impressed by Franky. She felt he was too quiet and would not make it as an account manager.

The position required a certain amount of assertiveness, especially when we were trying to convince a hiring manager to accept one of our contract therapists for thirteen weeks at seventy dollars an hour. A regular full-time employed therapist was earning only forty dollars an hour. But there was a shortage and, we tried to convince them, Ardor was the solution. We needed more help; demand was growing, and we did not have enough account managers to cover the country. And we wanted to have job opportunities in every state so as to continue to grow. We gave Franky a shot and agreed to hire him for $40,000 a year plus commission.

As the cliché reads, "the rest was history." Franky quickly set the gold standard for performance as an account manager. His bachelor's degree was in psychology, just like Stephanie's. He was persuasive and undaunted, just like Stephanie. As we listened to him on the telephone, we could hear that he did not like to accept no for an answer, as he pursued every conversation until he got his yes. His perseverance paid off handsomely. He became the first, and to date as of this writing, the only account manager to reach 100 working travelers in his book. And that was not enough because prior to Franky accepting a new position with the Stepping Stones Group at the time of our divestiture, he reached 125 working travelers.

We had many good times with him during his tenure. He was one of a few who joined us in New York at the president's club. He was on every cruise we took with our top producers. He was always quiet, almost shy at times, but his wit and his consummate success made him one of the special employees in our company's history. As of this writing, Franky remains with the Stepping Stones Group surely leading as a top producer.

2013

We now recognized a need to assemble a formal organizational chart with a CEO and president. In retrospect, we should have done this much sooner in our company's history. **BAD DECISION.**

Early in 2013 I assumed the role as CEO, Patty assumed the role as president, and we promoted Mikey to senior vice president in charge of sales. We righted the ship, and we were ready to get back to business. The disruption to our business caused when one of our key leaders left the organization was reflected as expected in our sales for 2012. There is no way to predict if or when a key leader will experience a change in attitude or habits. And there was no way for us to prepare for it. We could only deal with the consequence as best we could.

We closed the year with close to *$29 million* in sales. Although we lost Jimmy's leadership, the company grew. Now it was time for Mikey to spread his wing and guide us to our next threshold, *$50 million* in top-end sales.

It was in this new year that Mike and Patty went outside and sought consulting help. Our attorney, Roxanne knew a consultant who specialized in helping medical staffing companies achieve substantial growth. This was the first time we decided to follow the lead of a consultant. We did not want another bad outcome like our experience with Jimmy's leaving.

It was already getting late in the year when we hired Scott. Unfortunately, we may have waited too long to make the decision to bring Scott on board because we were experiencing sluggish sales and our sales staff were pointing fingers at each other rather than working together. It became apparent that it was not going to be as easy as we thought for Mikey to manage the entire team by himself. In one instance two of our top tenured recruiters asked for a closed-door meeting with us. In that meeting we were threatened that if we did not remove Mikey from authority, they were going to lead a walk-off for many of the staff. It was déjà vu all over again! The signs were clear now; we needed help.

KEY HIRE

Was there room for another Cody? We had already employed one of the friendliest and hardest-working accountants in the industry. But Robert applied for a position as an account Manager. And before he even completed his interview, every single female in the organization wanted to hire him. He was physically almost perfect with appealing hair and a soft but confident personality. Our account management team was large, but we made room for Robert.

As a team player he fit in perfectly and we came to learn quickly he was a natural coach. This trait was Robert's greatest strength. He unselfishly grew his business while looking out for other account managers and many of the recruiters. We made a **BAD DECISION** with Robert. As his tenure grew increasingly the staff looked to him for leadership. When it was decided that Monica was not up to the task as sales leader, Robert personally appealed to me and asked for a shot at the job. He went as far as to show me a job offer he had from a competitor with a leadership position at $150,000 a year. It was bad timing because we had already watched three internal employees fail at the position and had set our sights on hiring an outsider. Robert had ambitions that we did not recognize. When we rejected his request to replace Monica years later, he resigned his position with dignity.

2014

Our Cinderella story was ending. Once the books were closed for 2013, we were provided with the unwelcome news that our sales for the year had grown by less than $500,000. Our final top-line report measured total sales for 2013 of *$29,150,000*. As we celebrated our tenth year in operation and were now recognized as a midsized company, we should have been proud of where we were. And we were to some extent.

However, this was the first time in our company's ten-year history that we almost lost money. There was unrest among the staff, leadership was weakened, and we were scared. Fortunately, at this point we had fully engaged the consultant. He had spent many hours interviewing the staff and recording their thoughts and feelings about the direction of the company. In the end he provided us with a shocking report that recommended we release Mikey from his role and promote Sadie, one of our top producers who originally came on board when she left a large, publicly traded local medical staffing company. Sadie did have the background of having led a large team, and she was a married mom with two children equally respected by the entire sales staff.

This action was to become the most difficult one we had had to make since we founded the company. Mikey was our first hire in the sales department. He was not much older than our daughter, Stephanie. We treated him like a son. He respected us like parents. But he too agreed in the end that his tenure had run its course and he, like Jimmy, was ready to leave South Florida and relocate to Michigan, where he was born. In effect, we gave Mikey the opportunity to repatriate back home with enough money in his pocket to make that move financially possible.

Mikey had the same financial package with the same employment agreement as Jimmy. As an owner of 24 percent of the company stock he was entitled to his fair share. We were able to use the same valuation methodology we had used for Jimmy when we drew up Mikey's separation agreement. Mikey agreed to the same package Jimmy agreed to. Patty and I still remember the morning in a rented room at the Marriot Hotel when we met with Mikey and the consultant, Scott, and exchanged our goodbyes. We were all full of tears. This parting was going to be the toughest one to date.

An extremely positive event in 2014 proved to be one of the more significant events in the company's ten-year history. We hired a recruiter named Jacky who suggested we enter the business of placing our therapists in schools, versus placing them exclusively in healthcare facilities. We listened to Jacky as she crafted a plan that included hiring a recent MBA graduate to perform the tedious work of producing the requests for proposals that were necessary to gain the school contracts. Together they started securing contracts, initially in California, then in many of the Midwestern states. The most desired hires for these school districts were speech language pathologists. We learned quickly that any child who required speech assistance was entitled to this learning and the federal government would reimburse the schools. Over the course of the next seven years, leading up to the eventual sale of just the school placement business in October 2020, our team reached 225 school therapists actively working a full forty-two-week school year. This **GOOD DECISION** led to Mike and Patty's biggest business accomplishment to date.

It was also time that Mike and Patty increased their involvement with the operations, fearful that the enormous but unavoidable change in leadership may lead to another less-than-favorable revenue gain. Starting a new division was our first big step forward. Mike subscribed to a magazine called *Family Business*, and he caught the attention of a large home healthcare business located in New Jersey. After speaking with the founder a few times, we were both invited to visit their offices in New Jersey. Although we were unsuccessful at gaining any new business after our meeting, we felt rejuvenated about our company's direction. We decided to increase our marketing budget and approved the purchase of 1,000 mouse pads that we mailed to each of our clients around the holidays. Finally, we investigated partnering with other healthcare staffing companies for the first time to place our candidates in their open job assignments.

KEY HIRE

EMPLOYEE TWENTY

We were able to divest our school division in October 2020 because we had developed something unique that a private equity firm was willing to acquire. We were able to build that special division that catered to filling vacancies in school districts around the country with speech language pathologists because we had a special team that would stop at nothing short of success. We hired a special employee, Mary, who although just a newly minted MBA, wanted to make a splash. Mary's parents were also incredibly special. Both were very influential people in their home city of Guayaquil, Ecuador. Her mom was personally responsible for overseeing the Miss Universe pageant. Her mom invited Patty to come to her home country and help judge the contest. That was special.

We had a special relationship with Mary. We watched as she married, became a mom, and grew into a mature woman. We are thankful for this special one of our twenty-five employees and her loyalty to our company and our family over the years leading up to the sale of the school division. Not surprisingly, the private equity company would not move forward with a transaction by taking Mary for themselves. Today, she remains a key employee for the Stepping Stones Group.

KEY HIRE

Most of the employees we consider as one of the special *employees* fall into three categories. They are currently with us, they accepted positions with the Stepping Stones Group and continued as therapy placement specialists, or they left the company for growth opportunities with new firms.

Katie is still with us more than ten years later and is now responsible for all human resources and benefits administration. Her title is vice president, and what makes her extra special is that she supports the entire function without any full-time assistance. She worked her way up the organization over the years, initially as a sales assistant. Realizing her skills were not being maximized, we moved her into an administrative support position where she reported directly to Patty. Just before we left the South Florida market we promoted her to manager of administration, where she wore many hats. Soon after that we asked if we could send her for special training in human resources, where she showed real interest. Katie is married with a little boy and works remotely in Saint Augustine, Florida. She commutes regularly to our Tampa office and is now part of our exclusive leadership team that includes only our CEO, Stephanie, Mike, and Jenn.

2015

They say in Hollywood that the show must go on. It must be noted at this point that we were running a business. Although we had a private enterprise without any shareholders except Mike and Patty, our number one goal running the business was to make money for the shareholders, whether there 2 or 2,000. Something exceptionally good came from this action because we now had 100 percent of the company stock. It appeared to be a good decision at the time to give Mikey and Jimmy each a 24 percent stake in the company. Surely, it was a good motivational tool, or it appeared to be. But we should have been more conservative and distributed the shares over a period as the company grew. Coincidentally, it was not long after we distributed the shares that Jimmy, then Mikey's behavior changed. Distributing all that stock when and how we did it was a **BAD DECISION**.

We were thankful when 2014 was a rebound year. It appeared that following the advice of the consultant worked quite well. Our top-line revenue for the year was $35,283,000. We exceeded our expectations with our new leader in place and grew by an astonishing 50 percent. Sadie was rallying the team, and for the first time in the company's history we had a female overseeing the entire sales force, which was approaching thirty strong. The competition among the staff was healthy and we averaged more than thirty transactions most weeks.

Our school business was gaining steam rapidly. We learned there are more than 17,000 school districts in the United States. We had no idea how big of an opportunity we basically stumbled upon. And little did we know the new school division would sell in five short years and earn us a seven-figure payday.

The world was all right again, and we could not see any end to our rapid growth. And then, less than a year after we promoted her to a leadership position, Sadie approached us about buying the company. Patty and I were shocked at her request. We finally owned 100 percent of the company, and we were tracking toward that magical $50 million in revenue that would move us up to a large company category. Without too much though we told her no.

Patty and I were in Asheville, North Carolina, planning Stephanie's wedding. Our little girl was going to get married. We were living the dream. It was an amazing time for the family. Friends and family gathered for the once-in-a-lifetime event at the Biltmore Estate. On the drive home from the event, just the two of us with Stephanie's wedding dress hanging beautifully in the back seat, we received a phone call from Jenn, our manager of operations at the time. Shockingly, she advised us that Sadie, our sales leader, would be leaving the company and starting her own business based in Naples, Florida. By doing so she was in clear compliance with her noncompetition agreement, which stated she could work for another employer if that employer was fifty miles away from her current employer.

Patty and I had an epiphany. We had just trained an employee sufficiently to start her own staffing company and compete with us, all within the scope of her noncompetition agreement. And to make matters worse, she was the top-performing leader we had ever hired. But fortunately, we had become used to practicing what we preached, and we had a backup candidate in mind who could move right into her position.

Sadie left the company amicably. She was married and the breadwinner for her family. She was looking out for her family, and as family-first employers and people, we accepted her decision without malice. Unfortunately for us, our debut in Hollywood with our female star was too short-lived.

KEY HIRE

Over the course of close to twenty years we have had different banking relationships. For obvious reasons we chose banks based on location. We stayed loyal to our banks, especially when we had developed relationships with the bankers. <u>Having a bank that knew us by name was important</u>. The last bank we used, Bank of America, was located just across the street from our large top-floor office. Usually we found ourselves in the drive-through every couple of weeks, making deposits for the company.

Mike's mom always made sure she came to the window to take exceptional care of us. Sharon knew what business we were in and on multiple occasions, she asked us if we were hiring. Her son Mike was finishing his master's degree in accounting at FAU. After quite a few attempts, and with Mom's blessing, we were able to bring Mike in for an interview with Cody and the team. Yet another quiet unassuming personality, he was a hit.

Over the years Mike became Cody's right arm—another metaphor! They became another Ardor dynamic duo. At times they walked alike, talked alike, and dressed alike. Mike was the addition we did not know we needed to help us sustain our growth. Mike was so extraordinary at his interview with the Stepping Stones Group that he too became a condition of the transaction. Mike was truly a special employee.

2016

Again we found ourselves in charge of the organization, having to make decisions that would keep our growth plans alive. Gasoline prices were rising. We decided to award our sales staff with twenty-five-dollar gift cards from the corner Shell station. That was a **GOOD DECISION.** In another effort to keep our image fresh, we authorized a $10,000 upgrade to our website. And finally, to keep our internal recruitment efforts strong, we improved our commission structure.

By coincidence, our lease was ending and we were coming off our most successful year in the company's history. While Sadie was with us for that short period of time, we hired her husband along with another recruiter to start ArdorMD. That new division was established to focus on placing doctors in permanent positions soon after they were eligible for permanent employment. We did not have enough space for the new three-person team, so we had to secure another lease in the building next to us.

Our growing accounting team had also run out of space, and we rented additional space for that team across the hall in the same building. We had grown like wildfire, and we were bursting at the seams. Every desk was occupied in all three locations. My longtime friend Billy again came to the rescue. The top floor in our building was becoming available. It would require a significant down payment and a commitment to a five-year lease. The 17,000 square feet that were built out all brand-new for us came with a price tag of $50,000 a month. We did not have a CFO to convince me not to make the deal, so with Patty's blessing we signed the contract. **BAD DECISION.**

Over the course of our twelve-year history our rent went from $0 a month (the kitchen table) to an incredible $50,000 a month at our peak. That decision to lease that space was mostly motivated by the need for me to have the biggest office in town. A friend of ours who was operating a technical staffing company also wanted the space. I let my ego get the best of me!

Unlike Sadie, her replacement, Rob, did not work for the company as a recruiter. Rob was an account manager who focused primarily on securing contracts with new facilities and closing deals with the candidates submitted by the recruiters. At this point in our company's history we had twice as many recruiters as account managers. Rob had the support of all of his colleagues in his department, but he would have to earn the respect of the recruiting team that happened to be all women. His first year produced a gain in top-end sales of $1.5 million. The year 2015 was not a year for the record books, hardly the banner year that we saw in 2014. We closed the year at $36,750,000.

Again, we did have a growth year, but the pace of the growth would not support the liabilities we undertook when we moved into the new fourth-floor space. Patty and I started to worry again that we may be looking at a repeat of a few years before.

KEY HIRE

For more than ten years we have employed one individual who is still responsible for one of the more critical back-office functions of the company. When the office was operational in Coral Springs before the COVID-19 outbreak forced us to close the office, Melissa was one of the cheerleaders who kept everyone's spirits flying high.

Now she too worked in her home office most weeks, logging more than forty hours a week. On a weekly basis Melissa single-handedly generates all the invoices for our clients, emails those invoices individually to each of our clients, posts all of the cash that comes into the company, and maintains constant communication with our banks and customers for all billing matters. Melissa has also had over the years a special relationship with both of us. She is truly one of the family and continues to be one of the special twenty-five employees.

2017

It had been a little more than a year since Patty and I decided to sell our house in South Florida and follow our newly married daughter and her husband to Tampa. Patty had real reservations about making the move to Tampa, primarily because she was concerned about leaving the business with its current leadership team behind. And was she correct! For the first time since we opened our healthcare staffing business, we saw our top-end revenue decline. There was a lot of truth to the century-old saying that when the "cat's away the mice will play." Our revenue dropped by more than *$2.5 million* over 2015. Total sales for the year came in at an abysmal *$34,250,000*. Our EBITDA, the measurement on how our company would be valued, dropped more than *$1 million*. Our SG&A expenses were at their highest ever, morale was slipping again, and Rob told us that he wanted equity in the company. We were experiencing more bad news and thinking about selling the company. **GOOD DECISION**. We had been in contact with M&A consultants in the past, although not since 2009. Ironically, the group that helped facilitate our divestiture of the school business in 2020 had been trying to reach me for years, but I chose to ignore his calls mostly because the company was performing so well and we did not want to let it go. **BAD DECISION.** We should have started building a contact list of M&A consultants from day one. We may have been talking about our second sale now. Sales, general, and administrative expenses (SG&A) are all expenses not related to the cost of a company's production of goods or services.

KEY HIRE

Another Melissa had been an employee of Ardor Health Solutions for more than ten years. Her supervisor, Michael, said Melissa was homesick and wanted to relocate back to Naples—Florida, not Italy! She was only the second employee in the company's history who had asked to work remotely and Patty and I both were hesitant about approving the request. Little did we know that we were getting a peek into the future and that remote work would soon become more the norm than an exception.

Once Melissa set up her home office in Naples, she resumed her role as the only employee responsible for processing at one point more than 400 weekly time sheets. That tedious role sometimes meant she had to contact dozens of our traveling therapists and request they email their time sheets before the cutoff every Tuesday afternoon. Today we can proudly say that over the past ten years we have never missed payroll; every one of our external employees receives their pay on time every Friday. And because Melissa will work as many hours as necessary every week, we expect that we will never miss a payroll.

2018

History has a habit of repeating itself. Bell-bottoms are back in style, as is long hair for boys and jeans we used to call high waters. When fashion trends repeat no one is harmed, and if you are smart enough to hang on to your old clothes you are fashionable immediately. However, when bad events repeat themselves, the outcomes could be horrible. This was the case for Mike and Patty in 2018.

Rob did decide to leave the company, and he took several of our employees with him. Because we were not managing the business as closely as we should have, he was able to circumvent his noncompetition agreement and start his staffing company less than fifty miles from our corporate location.

We really paid a high price believing the company would continue to thrive even though we were not onsite or at least in the same city providing the necessary oversight. Rob was the second consecutive leader we put in place who then promptly left our company and started a competing company. We had to review our employment agreements. If we had agreements that were more bulletproof, it is possible that Sadie and Rob would not have left. **BAD DECISION**.

Our leadership bench was exhausted. We had a plan and it was executed perfectly when Mikey left the company. That year the company grew by almost *$6 million*. But when Sadie left and we promoted Rob to replace her, our revenue growth slowed to *$1.5 million*. And now with a replacement for Rob in place who we were not sure had the necessary experience to lead the team, our revenue for 2017 dropped precipitously by *$3 million*. We closed 2017 with a top-line revenue of *$31,250,000*. And more concerning was the fact that our EBITDA that year dropped all the way down to *$500,000*. At our peak in 2015 our EBITDA was close to *$3 million*.

At a multiple of seven times earnings our company would have been valued at $21 million.[5] At the end of 2017 our company would probably have been valued at *$2 million*, in part because when EBITDA drops so does the multiple. Our desire to sell the company was growing exponentially.

---

5   Multiple is used in calculating the enterprise value of a company. For example, a company with an EBITDA of $2 million that can fetch a multiple of seven is worth $14 million potentially.

2019

Merry-go-rounds are fun. We remember not long ago when our oldest granddaughter, Isabella, first experienced the merry-go-round. As the white horse she chose went up and down and round and round she smiled and said in an ever-so-low tone, "Up-and-Down." But the ups and downs on the metaphorical merry-go-round of business are nowhere near as fun. In fact, they are potentially disastrous. Our carousel of leadership ups and downs saw Sadie replace Mikey, who had been in a key leadership role for ten years, then Rob replaced Sadie after just over one year, and now Lana was replacing Rob after just one year. And it was not completely shocking when Lana and the two of us realized she was not up for the task either, despite her 100 percent effort. The year was another disappointment. We closed out 2018 at just more than *$30 million* in sales. We finally realized our internal staff of possibly qualified leaders was tapped out. It was time to go outside and look for someone who could get the company back on the growth track we were used to. We hired a woman who had more than twenty years of experience in medical staffing in a leadership role. CeeCee arrived in her giant pickup truck towing a massive fifth wheel. She was a Texan who was working remotely for a local company. She was willing to leave her mobile apartment in Tampa, where we were now starting to add local staff, and travel to South Florida weekly to meet with the now remote staff in hotel boardrooms. Her résumé was impressive; she appeared to be just what the doctor ordered.

Unfortunately, again, we made a **BAD DECISION**. CeeCee was not healthy enough to perform the routine trips we needed to ensure the success of her employment. And as a result, the staff were unwilling to accept her as a leader. She resigned early in 2019.

We did, however, avert yet another bad decision in 2019. Soon after we started the company in 2004 we had made a conscious decision to build rather than buy our information systems. There were few offers at that time for specific software solutions written for the medical staffing industry. And because I had an extensive background in programming the decision made sense to the entire team. Now almost fifteen years later, with the help of the same developer who started the project, MedTrak had become a robust system that connected seamlessly with our accounting and payroll software. But there was an itch to move into the temporary nurse staffing business. And our MedTrak solution was not programmed to help us solve the problem. We reached out to several software providers and decided to go with a company that specialized allegedly in temporary nurse staffing.

What a mistake we made and what a **BAD DECISION** we averted when we decided after almost one year of effort and tens of thousands of dollars trying to affect a conversion from our homegrown software to an off-theshelf solution. Our revenue in 2019 was tracking on a similar trajectory to our revenue almost ten years previously. We created an unnecessary distraction at probably the worse time possible.

2020

If we learned anything since the year we had our planned leadership change, it is that you must stay prepared for the unpredictable. We had some comfort level when we hired CeeCee; she was an outsider with much more staffing experience than any of her predecessors. In retrospect, we rushed into the decision again because we were no longer operating locally in the South Florida market. Again we were faced with a decision to fill that same leadership role that had been vacated every year since 2013. We looked toward the one employee who had taken command of our school division. That division now accounted for more than one-half of our business. It seemed logical to pull that resource at this time of need.

The staff was jubilant when we announced that Mary, a young MBA student hired years before, was now going to succeed as the leader of our sales organization. By now the group had grown to thirty total employees. Maria had the management experience she earned academically, and she was performing leadership although unofficially over a small team generating more than $15 million in revenue. After Maria, we were running out of skilled employees we could even consider for the job.

Mary was going to be the sixth person assuming the leadership role in seven years. Fortunately for us, although we were experiencing the very worst times since we started the company in 2004, Patty and I were attentive enough to realize that the honeymoon, at least with this group of employees performing therapy staffing, was coming to a bittersweet end.

By the time 2020 began, again the beginning of a new decade, we were immersed in a due diligence process with a private equity group.[6] We had stayed in close contact with an M&A advisory group, and they introduced us to a prospective buyer interested in acquiring all the assets of the company. The group was well funded and its original founders were European with business experience that dated back to the 1800s. Over the years we had flirted with several prospects, but we never made it into a due diligence period.

What we did not know because, again, this was our first time going down this road, was that the due diligence period would be incredibly time-consuming and the depth of the buyers' audits mirrored a process that could be aligned with that of the IRS.

Admittedly, after spending close to one year in the process we were getting discouraged. At the same time, I was spending most of my day every day responding to different requests from the buyers' seven audit groups and our daily sales results were continuing to trend downward. Then suddenly the buyers announced they were only interested in acquiring the school business in a stock sale.[7]

That meant that after the transaction closed, Patty and I and Stephanie and Mike would still own the remaining part of the company that was not involved in placing therapists in school districts. At first, we were not sure it was a good idea,

---

6 Typically, the due diligence process begins shortly after both parties agree to complete a transaction. In our case the buyers used outside consulting services to audit every part of the business that would be included in the transaction.

7 In this case we created a new company called Ardor School Solutions and moved only the assets related to that division of the company, leaving the remaining parts of Ardor behind in the ownership of the family.

especially since we had plans to fully liquidate the assets of the company and possibly retire. If this scenario were to move forward, our children and most of the remaining employees would still have jobs. It did not take long for us to consider the pros and the cons. If the deal were to close, I would say that repeatedly because in business, until the wire hits the bank you cannot count on it.

We were already past the second quarter of the year and now the diligence efforts were strictly related to the school business, which allowed us some free time to contemplate what Ardor would look like with the school division. It was during those conversations primarily with Stephanie and Mike and a few of our key leaders that we started to discuss placing registered nurses along with therapists. We could no longer make placements in school districts anywhere in the United States as a condition of our sale. That was okay and it seemed reasonable enough at the time. We would have to focus on hospitals if we wanted to stay in business.

As we closed out the third quarter and were now more than fifteen months into the due diligence period, we received a sign that the deal was finally going to happen. Our primary buyer contact, another named Mike from Massachusetts, told me the CEO, Tim, said the diligence process had consumed enough time and resources and he had to get the deal closed ASAP. On October 10, 2020, Patty and I sat in our attorney's office in Tampa as we waited for the final signed and countersigned agreements to come across via email. The eventual document, of which we also received a hard copy, filled a four-inch binder. All that exhausting work was captured for our eyes to see.

When the project was finally labeled as complete, we had agreed to allow the buyers to hire all the key sales staff who worked exclusively in the school division. Additionally, they hired our junior controller. In total thirteen of our employees became part of the transaction. This request was a blessing because in our new company that would be generating significantly less revenue without the school division, we would be able to continue to operate without borrowing extra capital. We used $1 million from the proceeds to pay off the debt we had borrowed during COVID-19 when we were paying our school therapists but unable to bill for them.

The year 2020 turned out to be one of the best years for us personally since we started our first company back in the year 2000. We were now fully operational in Tampa with money in the bank and were excited about the prospect of doing it again!

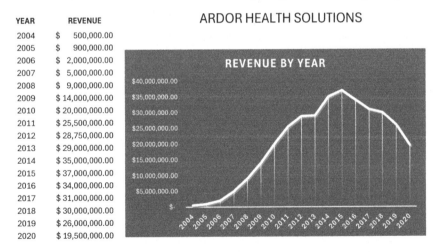

YEAR	REVENUE
2004	$ 500,000.00
2005	$ 900,000.00
2006	$ 2,000,000.00
2007	$ 5,000,000.00
2008	$ 9,000,000.00
2009	$ 14,000,000.00
2010	$ 20,000,000.00
2011	$ 25,500,000.00
2012	$ 28,750,000.00
2013	$ 29,000,000.00
2014	$ 35,000,000.00
2015	$ 37,000,000.00
2016	$ 34,000,000.00
2017	$ 31,000,000.00
2018	$ 30,000,000.00
2019	$ 26,000,000.00
2020	$ 19,500,000.00

LEADERSHIP REALLY MAKES A DIFFERENCE WHEN GROWING A LARGE COMPANY

THE DECLINES WE EXPERIENCED STARTING IN 2016 WERE TIED DIRECTLY
TO THE BAD DECISIONS WE MADE FOR THE TOP LEADERSHIP POSITION
OUR DECLINES WERE FURTHER ACCELERATED STARTING IN 2019 BY THE COVID-19 OUTBREAK

IV. HOW YOU CAN DO IT: WORKING TOGETHER

ACT FIVE. YOUR SPOUSE IS YOUR GREATEST PARTNER

Chick Hearn, a well-known sports announcer for the Los Angeles Lakers, said it is hard to argue with success. That's how he described the year-over-year outstanding performance of the basketball team for which he called play-by-plays for many years.

Mike's dad ran a successful upholstery business for more than two decades. He had one partner, my mother, Lucy. My mom answered the phones because back in the 1960s we had party lines in Brooklyn and although the phone rang in Dad's store, it also rang in our apartment almost one mile away. As the business grew Dad hired Mrs. Nash, a tenant in his smaller apartment building, to answer the phones and set appointments. But otherwise Dad did it all. He picked up the furniture that needed recovering. Working with Bill, they prepared the replacement fabric, usually leatherette, which he referred to as fireproof, waterproof, and crackproof. Dad did all the sewing. Bill completed the process. Later, while still in grade school, I was taught to coat the wooden legs of the furniture with Old English. As I grew stronger, I would help Dad put the recovered furniture in the truck and then off we went to make the delivery. That was the simple family-run process.

I remember seeing different faces over the years in the store, but none were ever elevated to partner. Of course, by now the reader knows Patty and Mike did not have the best experiences with our partners toward the end. Our partners did play a pivotal role in growing the company in our early years, but disagreements led to down years and ultimately the break-up of what was originally something special.

We learned a very difficult lesson during our business-building years. Outside partnerships can be great and helped lead us to extraordinary growth, **but waking up and going to bed with a partner who shares your values** and interest in success is better than coupling up with friends or strangers who you may not see eye to eye with in the end.

If you are starting your business new you can make this decision. If you have already started your business and have a partner, we hope there are enough teaching moments in our book that will benefit you and keep you from making bad decisions.

ACT SIX. HOW WE BEAT ADVERSITY

At no time will you read in this or any other book that building a business is easy. If you do read that comment in another book, close it, then burn it because it is far from the truth. Over the close to twenty-year period during which built our business from scratch, we were forced to deal with problems we did not ever imagine. Some of those problems were easily solved in an hour or two only because we were agile enough to make quick decisions without convening a larger group of leaders and having useless discussions. At other times, the problems were not so easily solved and the timeline for corrections spanned several months.

A good plan violently executed now is better than a perfect plan executed next week.

~George S. Patton

Lightning Struck

We decided to open our first company not far from the home we lived in at the time. It was our first new home, an incredibly beautiful four-bedroom pool home on a lake. Our drive to work was pleasant because our first office was in front of the home in our home office. We were in Coral Springs, which although it is not the lightning capital of the world, at times it deserves the honor. And before we stopped operating from our home, as luck would have it, lightning did strike. We lost our main computer to an electric surge and sustained a fair amount of roof damage. But with our tenacity we replaced, rebuilt, and moved on.

The Hurricane

We consciously decided to stay in South Florida as we moved into our first office, then a bigger office, and yet again a bigger office. Everyone knows Florida and now much of the gulf coast and the Atlantic coast are very prone to hurricanes. Similarly, the northeast is known for sometimes violent winter storms that can knock power out for days at a time. And of course, the middle of the country is mostly susceptible to killer tornados. With all that in mind, many of the major staffing companies like us are in the state of Florida, disproportionally on the east coast of Florida. And many of the larger staffing companies are also located in Nebraska in tornado alley.

As business owners we take a risk when we decide to open our doors in otherwise unwelcoming locations. We did accept that risk and, boy, did we ever pay for it. Late in 2005, just as we were closing out our second full year of operations at Ardor Health Solutions, a storm named Wilma that spent more than a week spinning over the Yucatan Peninsula began heading north into the Gulf of Mexico. All the hurricane models projected that the storm would continue to track north along Florida's west coast and eventually make landfall far north of us. This was when adversity struck a second time. Without warning the storm turned toward the east at the same exact latitude as our building and hit us head on. We received a direct hit from a category three hurricane; we were not prepared. All of our systems were local to our facility. We went down hard—no electricity, no internet, no telephone, and limited running water.

Before it was over—and we were thankful the storm ushered in a cold front because we had no air conditioning—we set up a makeshift office on the bare concrete floor of our home that was under renovation. Earlier in the year we had decided to remove the old floor tile from our recent purchase in Parkland and replace it with imported Italian marble. As we began to assemble our disaster team of key employees, we had to move the cement mixer that was in the kitchen to make room for tables and chairs. It was payday like any other week, and because our employees were mostly out of state, we had no way to contact anyone. We did not want to miss a payroll. We were able to gain access to our building long enough to grab envelopes, checks, and stamps. Using the prior week's payroll reports Patty started handwriting payroll checks. With the assistance of two other employees, we sat in our dusty house, dimly lit by only the sunshine.

We were just two years into our new medical staffing company and this event was the greatest adversity that as a team we had to overcome. We even had enough information to process accounts payables.

The fire and then the flood

It was common to allow the burning of live candles at our employees' desks. The fact that our workforce was made up mostly of women was more reason to allow live candles to burn. Some mornings we would walk through our new larger offices and enjoy different scents such as vanilla, strawberry, watermelon, and coconut. It was yet another morale booster that did not cost the company or the owners any extra money. Patty on occasion even purchased the candles and used them as incentives to increase productivity.

Well, our decision to allow this practice came full circle one early spring morning. I can still remember standing outside and feeling the need for a sweater or jacket when the fire trucks started arriving.

Karen, one of our top-producing recruiters, had a sweater draped around her chair most of the time. We kept the offices cold to keep our employees alert. At nine o'clock sharp one Monday morning we all huddled for our normal first meeting of the week in the conference room. As usual, all the candles were lit and the aroma filled the air. However, this morning, when she pushed her chair back to leave for the meeting, her sweater caught fire. We did not recognize what happened until the fire sprinkler over her desk started spraying water. Not surprisingly, that triggered a second sprinkler, then another, then another. Meanwhile, the fire started to spread into other cubicles. Panic filled the office and Jimmy stood up and ordered everyone to get out.

It took more than three months for our operations to return to normalcy. Not only did the disaster affect our area, but the water also dripped down through two floors and affected every other tenant below us. They were not happy.

Less than a year later we were presented with an opportunity to upgrade our space and move into a new building. Fortunately, our new neighbors had no knowledge of what had happened at our previous location.

Raining down on the first floor

Years later, one Friday night we were wrapping up another good week. Mike was still working closely with the sales team, trying to get to thirty placements before shutting down for the weekend. It was not just raining outside; it was pouring. I remember spending my high school days in Miami in the mid-1970s. I would set my Seiko watch every day for three o'clock when the rain would start. And, as usual, by no later than four o'clock the rain would stop, the sun would come back out, and it would get extremely hot again. One of the reasons Patty and I decided to leave Miami after we were married was to find some reprieve from the heat. Broward County did offer that reprieve, especially since we were so far west in Coral Springs. The downside to that location was that it seemed to rain, not once a day for one hour, but all day and every day.

This Friday was no exception. Our home telephone rang. Mikey said that water was pouring in through the ceiling. Trey was in in corner, in a great and fun mood as usual. We heard him yelling for attention, "Come save us, bring a lifeboat!"

Patty and I purposely bought our house in an area that also supported commercial real estate, so we made our way to the office in five minutes. Together with the team of ten who were still in the office late that Friday night we moved all of the equipment from the back part of the office where the water was penetrating, relocated all the personal belongings from the desks that were in danger of getting wet, and used trash bags to cover everything and anything that was not already soaked. I immediately notified the management company and we waited for assistance. This time only two months later, our operation was back to normal. And once again, we overcame diversity with our hard work and undaunted attitudes.

COVID-19: A last note on adversity

Years before the COVID-19 pandemic struck in the United States there was a trend toward working remotely. Our leadership team tried hiring employees from different parts of the country to take advantage of talent that existed outside our small county in Florida. And each time we decided to hire a remote worker, it failed. We have come to learn that the most important thing missing was the technology to support and monitor those remote workers. Now, years after the pandemic was declared over, we employ that technology across the entire organization.

The mandate by Broward County to close our offices seemed like it was going to be the biggest challenge in our company's history. Everyone was using desktop computers. One of our QuickBooks accounting systems was cloud based. Where would our employees set up workstations? Not everyone, not even some, had home offices. As usual, although now with the help of a more mature and experienced leadership team, we sprang into action. We equipped each employee one by one with access to high-speed internet. When necessary, we purchased small tables or desks they could place their equipment on. We offered to pay for all office items they needed to create a working remote environment. Our company came back to life, productivity returned, and we even saw improvements in some areas.

Our 17,000-square-foot office, where we had plans to house more than 200 employees ahead of the pandemic, never reopened. We experienced some retention loss. We experienced more unplanned increases in sales from our top producers. And then we decided to open a much smaller, 2,000-square-foot office in Tampa, where our growing family would live.

ACT SEVEN. HOW TO IDENTIFY CONSULTANTS AND CON ARTISTS

A famous German philosopher named Friedrich Nietzsche said we are only as strong as our weakest link. When Patty and Mike started their company, there were only two of them. And trust us, we were far from the smartest people to ever start a business. For that reason and for many more, early on we were faced with a decision to hire consultants to help us overcome the normal challenges that confront first-time business owners. Two types of consultants we were forced to hire early on were accountants and attorneys. Both professionals should help business owners save money. And although you may think all accountants and attorneys will be honest and helpful, that is not the case. What follows is a narrative of our experiences over the twenty years that led up to our eventual sale of part of our company.

NEWS FLASH! If you have a business that will require a physical structure, not a business that will utilize remote workers, deploy cameras! In more than one instance several of our consultants and employees who became con artists and hurt our cause would have been stopped had we deployed cameras throughout the building.

ONE

Our first consultant helped us make a lot of money in the beginning. That should be your criteria before you hire a consultant. Can we make money by agreeing to hire a consultant? Is there an alternative? Earlier we mentioned that one of our top recruiters discovered an opportunity when she recruited a physical therapist who needed sponsorship. Ray, who at that time was Stephanie's employer, was an immigration attorney in Fort Lauderdale. Although he specialized in helping people immigrate into the United States from Canada, he said he would lend us a hand. We immediately figured out that we could put his costs inside our gross profit calculations and pass those costs over to our hiring managers.

Ray showed up and in a big way. When we ended the program many years later because of a change in the laws, Ray had helped Mia place more than fifty physical therapists on two-year assignments. Those contracts were valued at more than $240,000 each, close to fifteen years ago. Imagine what they would have been worth in today's dollars.

GOOD DECISION. Consider what you are specializing in. Search your local market first for experts who can help you rapidly monetize your ideas. If it were not for Ray, we would have missed the opportunity to generate more than $10 million in revenue.

TWO

Our second consultant hired was our corporate attorney. Roxanne's office was nearby in downtown Ft. Lauderdale. She worked for a prestigious firm in a glamorous building, and she had a long history of providing sound advice to small business owners like us. Over many years Roxanne advised us on matters of employment and contract law. She was instrumental in developing our original employment agreements, our noncompete agreements and our client contracts. Roxanne introduced us to many of the consultants we hired over the first ten years of our company's existence. We believe it would be very prudent to find and hire a good corporate lawyer for your business, especially one who has specific expertise in your industry, which in our case is staffing.

THREE

Our third outside consulting hire was our CPA, Sandy. Sandy's firm was a smaller boutique CPA firm that operated locally out of Boca Raton. It was important that our CPA was located a short driving distance from our corporate attorney. Business owners often meet their key consultants in person and discuss critical issues privately. Hiring Sandy as our CPA was one of the best hires we ever made. Sandy's firm was present throughout the growth of our company as we expanded into more than forty states and then were expected to file tax returns in all forty states. He and his colleagues made sure we stayed compliant not only at the federal level but also at the state level, where some requirements can be extremely difficult. Recently Sandy's firm was acquired by a private equity group. And because of that merger, Sandy's team has expanded and more expertise has been made available to us. How **GOOD WAS THE DECISION** to hire Sandy? He is still our CPA more than twenty years later.

FOUR

Training the sales teams was the responsibility of Mikey and Jimmy. Hiring well-qualified sales leaders is critical to any business and can make all the difference in the world with the speed in which you grow. We were fortunate enough to achieve explosive growth from year one, growing most years at more than 100 percent year over year. However, our highly motivated sales force grew bored of the same old motivational speeches Mikey and Jimmy delivered every single day at 8:30 a.m. We needed to find a way to keep the momentum going.

At a Staffing Industry Analysts meeting early in our history, Patty sat in a session with a sales trainer named Don. After that session she was quick to report that Don was extremely articulate and charismatic and she thought he was worth pursuing as a sales trainer for our company. Before we left the annual meeting we met with Don and decided to give him a shot. Our decision to bring on this third outside consultant was a very good decision. Don started flying in from his home city of Atlanta once quarterly to address our staff. I sometimes met Don for breakfast ahead of his day-long sessions and got his opinions on how our sales staff were implementing his recommendations. He became a key addition to our full-time trainers, Mikey, and Jimmy, because he provided an outside and unbiased opinion of our sales staff. Tim, as our first consultant, helped us generate the profits necessary to pay for our outside consultants. Don paid for himself. He helped us grow to a $30 million company in ten years.

FIVE

In 2013, Roxanne introduced us to our next outside consultant. As previously written, we were experiencing our first disruption in our business since inception, and it was tied to a failure of leadership. Patty and I were at a loss when this matter was initially presented to us, and it made perfect sense to reach out to our corporate council for an opinion. It should be noted that every time we did reach out to our lawyer the meter started running. At that time, we were only paying a meager

$250 per hour. Anecdotally, our normal legal fees are closer to $500 per hour. So we always thought twice about reaching out for a consultation.

Roxanne referred us to Steve, a staffing consultant also Florida based. He was also the second consultant we hired who was not remote to our location, which meant that in addition to hourly fees, we paid for travel time. Patty and I met with Steve over several months and discussed our issues. He concluded that we did have a leadership issue and that Mikey, one of our first hires from 2003, was the root cause of the problem and we should consider offering him a severance package to leave the organization. Although the decision to part ways with Mikey and promote his top recruiter to a leadership position seemed best at the time, it turned out to be a **BAD DECISION**.

At that point in our company's history, we exceeded all our competitors in the therapy space. We placed more therapists on thirteen-week assignments every week than other publicly traded companies. We became known as the therapy source. But we wanted to break into nursing. Over the years Patty and I had approached Mikey about expanding our business into nursing, which at the time was the largest segment of medical staffing in the United States. And there was plenty of room for more competition such as Ardor Health Solutions. Unfortunately, Mikey had no interest in abandoning his favorite segment for another. The **BAD DECISION** surfaced when we realized that we should have kept Mikey in the Therapy Division and replaced the staff he disagreed with and offered Sadie a position of leadership.

We had recruited Sadie from the largest nurse staffing company in the country, where she had more than 100 nurses working for her. Mikey and Sadie got along great and would have been a complementary team heading up our Therapy and Nursing divisions. Steve should have made that observation and made that recommendation. The ultimate outcome of our decision to terminate Mikey and replace him with Sadie was disastrous because just a little more than a year after we promoted her, she left the company and started her own medical staffing company. Hiring Steve ended up being a **BAD DECISION**.

SIX

Our revenue continued to grow after Sadie left the company, but at an anemic rate. Under Sadie's leadership we experienced a $6 million year-over-year annual growth. When she quit, we immediately reached out to the next best salesperson to head up the sales team. But that decision also turned out to be a *bad decision*. Again Patty and I were faced with adversity we were not prepared to repair without outside help. We turned once again to Roxanne, who promptly referred another industry heavyweight. After several meetings and partly out of desperation, we decided to hire Kurt in a consultant role. Rob increased the revenue by less than $1 million in his first year as the sales leader. We were not at all pleased with his performance. Kurt suggested we implement some of the metric and key performance indicators (KPIs) he used from his former employer. He spent most of his time as a highly paid consultant to the company working directly with Rob, in part coaching him to become a better leader. When Kurt's contract with us ended after approximately one year, we had spent more than $100,000 on his fees.

SEVEN

While Kurt was actively consulting with us, we had increased concerns that our data was being stolen. We were not sure by whom, but for some reason our sales were continuing to slow and our cancellation rate with our therapists was on the rise. Current employees could easily export lists of our therapists and share them with former employees. Kurt was aware that this was more commonplace than we thought and promptly referred an investigator to help solve the mystery. And yes, this was another **BAD DECISION**.

The investigator who worked with Kurt at his previous firm was expensive and his findings were inconclusive. We were working on a hunch that someone was out to get us, but it was not the case. Although Rob, our new leader, was the first employee the investigator, John, cleared of any wrongdoing, unfortunately, it was Rob who ended up leaving the company the following year and competing directly with us.

EIGHT

Kurt also suggested our marketing programs were inadequate and outdated, and he referred a close colleague, Tim, who had experience in that area. Tim was enthusiastic about starting a consulting assignment with Ardor. He also had an impressive list of current and former clients. In a short period of time, Jim redesigned all our marketing materials and convinced us to acquire a blow-up booth we could use at our conferences. We were paying airlines hundreds of dollars to transport bulky suitcases that were outdated every time we attended a conference. It seemed like a good idea; surely it would easier to transport than the traditional booth. No one ever mastered the art of constructing the new booth in a reasonable time at the conference.

When we wrapped up our consulting contract with Tim, we found thousands of printed documents we could hand out to prospects and an inflatable booth no one ever wanted to take to the annual conferences. We did not need to spend this money on a new marketing campaign we never used. We hired another consultant we did not need. We made another **BAD DECISION.**

NINE

Kurt joined the company at our most turbulent time. In three short years we had three leadership changes and Patty and I were convinced it was time to stop promoting salespeople we thought would make good leaders. The fact that someone in your organization is extremely talented in their technical roles does not qualify them for leadership positions. Kurt had a long list of colleagues since he had been working locally in the healthcare staffing sector as a leader for some time. He introduced us to a former employee of his who he thought would be a very good fit for our company. Desperation was surrounding us and we needed to move fast, so we allowed Kurt's referral to come in and meet with the team. While I was collaborating with the attorneys formalizing a draft offer letter for our next leader, John was making a presentation to the sales team. What happened in the next hour would normally be considered impossible.

John had made some disparaging remarks during his presentation to a mostly female staff about their interest in him. What followed was even more distressing. Because John and his lawyer interpreted his verbal employment agreement as legal, we had to make a six-figure payment to John in order to avoid going to court. As unbelievable as it appeared, we made our third **BAD DECISION** in a row.

TEN

Patty and I had to believe given our optimistic view of the world that at some point our luck would change. We had worked our way through the COVID-19 outbreak, our employees were all remote, we were able to break our lease, and the general attitude of our staff was returning to normal. The biggest change that came our way occurred when we finally closed the transaction on our school therapy business. As a result of that transaction, we were able to reduce the size of our internal staff, which included accounting, and hire an outside firm to perform that function. Hiring Susan's firm to perform all our accounting functions was a **GOOD DECISION**.

Prior to the transactions we employed two full-time employees to perform our accounting functions at a cost of close to $200,000 a year. Once we outsourced the function, we reduced our spend by 100 percent and we gained the expertise of more than a dozen qualified accountants to perform daily inputs, weekly cash flow reports, and monthly closings along with quarterly, semiannual, and annual reporting. Susan and her firm remain with Ardor today, and we expect to maintain that relationship well into the future until we divest our company again.

V. WHAT WE COULD HAVE DONE DIFFERENTLY

ACT EIGHT. LIFESTYLE BUSINESS VERSUS BUILT TO SELL

The thought of selling our company never crossed our minds in the spring of 2000. Although we were doing much better financially then we ever had in our now twenty years and six months of married life, we were still working for someone else. We did finally manage to save some money, and when we sold our house in Miami, we were able to save a few more dollars. But Mike wanted more, and he was always convincing Patty that more was possible and inevitable. Part of Patty's intrigue about Michael was that we were always positive. And I still am today twenty-four years later. Things happen and happen for a reason. When our new concert hall Yamaha C7 piano was not delivered yesterday, we both agreed that it was not meant to be.

The conversations that started in late 1999 that became more frequent in 2000 were all about figuring out a way to get ahead—to start our own business. The planets were lining up for us nightly. Stephanie was preparing to start her first semester that summer so she could gain admission to the University of Central Florida. Mike was graduating from eighth grade at Saint John Neuman Catholic School and would have to transfer to a Catholic high school that would require much more commuting than Patty was used to. And because Mike was leaving for high school, Patty was no longer at school working with her children. The last one, unfortunately, was gone. And perhaps the tipping point came when Mike looked at his diminishing client list and realized he was preparing to start the cycle working for his employer all over again.

We owned a small Lexus SUV. Patty drove it most of the time and allowed Stephanie to use it on occasion. Mike was driving a Ford Taurus, not by choice, which was all we could afford. But Stephanie needed a car for college. The UCF campus was sprawling, and a car would absolutely be necessary. Spring was approaching. Our children's graduations would be just one day apart from each other that May. We were ready.

We had been looking in Broward County at a new house. If we could sell our house in Miami for a small profit, I knew I could make it work. But I would still be an employee, and Patty would not have a job. Mike wanted to buy a nice foreign sedan. He felt we deserved it. This is where the lifestyle business comes into play.

We both grew up with minimal luxuries, mostly necessities. And after twenty years of marriage, things were not very different. All of our vacations were local. We never left the country. Mike especially had a thirst for a better life, perhaps a trip to Europe with the kids, or a vacation to the mountains. Mike never even considered building a company to flip it. If that is your intention, then the plans for new cars and luxurious vacations will not materialize.

Soon after we started HighTechGroup in 2000, we leased a new Lexus LS. We needed it to chauffeur our clients, didn't we? Of could we have continued with Mike's Ford Taurus. <u>*That was a lifestyle choice*</u>. Our CFO, if we had one, would never have approved of that acquisition. And we needed a higher salary to support our new lifestyle, so we doubled it as soon as the company made enough profit. Our CFO would not have approved of that decision either. We hired Stephanie, then eventually Mike part-time to help with office tasks we used to do. <u>*Again, a lifestyle choice*</u>.

It has been twenty-four years since either of us has worked for someone else. And in hindsight we would not have changed a thing. We had a liquidation event in 2020, slightly more than fifteen years after we founded Ardor Health Solution. Our children now forty-two and thirty-nine are in the C suite of our company reporting to a new CEO who is not a family member. We remain on the payroll and have excellent health insurance the company pays for, as do Stephanie and Mike. There are many reasons to start and build a lifestyle company. However, there are several very good reasons to start and build a company purposely to sell it. I recall a conversation I had with another tenant in one of our buildings years ago. He told me that since he started his first company many years ago his plan was to hold the company for two to three years then sell it, even if the company was doing poorly. Of course he was a brilliant entrepreneur, so he always made money. He would then place some of his proceeds into savings and start another company. He did not drive a luxury vehicle and his children were not on his payroll. Every penny his company made he put back into the company to expand it, for the purpose of selling it one day.

His partner had a financial background and filled the role of CFO. Had we followed this scenario we could have built and sold five, six, or seven times over. Of course there is that one small matter one would have to survive every two or three years. That includes finding a buyer, successfully entering, and exiting a successful due diligence process, and closing the deal. And after close to eighteen months of that same process just one time, we are happy with our decision to build a lifestyle company.

ACT NINE. WE COULD HAVE SOLD OUR FIRST BUSINESS

We kept operating HighTechGroup mostly in a part-time fashion throughout most of 2004. By then all the former employees had found other positions. We did not hold anyone accountable to their noncompetes because we had decided to stop operating the company. We gave Chris an opportunity to transition to a healthcare recruiter, but it was not his passion – a **BAD DECISION**.

We could have promoted Chris to a leadership role with HighTechGroup and allowed him to keep doing what he had a passion for, IT recruiting. We could have kept Dana, who left because she saw we were shifting our focus to healthcare, and promoted her to a leadership role in account management. Instead, we slowly stopped filling open orders and eventually we stopped the operations.

Alternatively, we could have sold HighTechGroup. Why not? Our startup was just entering its prime in 2001 when 9/11 hit. We ended 2001 with *$1,000,000.00* in sales. We had all the components in place a buyer would have been looking for: a good, experienced team, with close to twenty years of experience collectively. All of them were willing to continue to work. Mike and Patty would have been willing to stay behind for the usual mandatory year buyers want. Although the market softened temporarily in 2002 an absolute rebound started in 2003 and never stopped. And, most important, HighTechGroup had a very respectable EBITDA.[8]

Our EBITDA for the year 2002 was $500,000. And although we decided in 2003 to shift away from IT staffing and move toward healthcare staffing, we did create a budget for 2003 that included doubling our sales by hiring another recruiter and another outside account manager. We also forecast that our existing customers might resume some of their hiring and potentially expand. Our budget for 2003 would have been achievable. And if we had made the choice to pursue the business of staffing IT for one more year, our sales would have surpassed $2 million and our EBITDA could have reached $1 million. This fact is most important because it is how a potential buyer values a business.

In the 2020s ahead of the COVID-19 pandemic, larger IT staffing companies were valued at multiples of ten times or greater.[9] Had we decided to build the business for one more year, it is possible that with $1 million in EBITDA, and a multiple

---

8   EBITDA is defined as earnings before interest tax depreciation and amortization.
9   A multiple is a value that is assigned by a buyer when calculating the enterprise value of a company. The enterprise value of a company is computed by multiplying EBITDA times the multiple.

offered by a buyer just five times, we could have sold our first business for $5 million. With that in mind, there are many ifs that go along with that assumption. In the very beginning we noted that **_selling a business is hard._** So rather than look back at what might have been, good entrepreneurs must always look ahead and live with their past decisions.

In conclusion, we have met business owners who build a business and sell it every three years. Steve was one of them. He told us when he was looking at our company as a potential purchaser that he would sell his business every three years even if it were losing money. We did not choose that path and we still have our business after twenty-plus years. And we are incredibly happy that we made that choice. **GOOD DECISION.**

ACT TEN. WE COULD HAVE BUILT AND SOLD ARDOR FASTER

In the year 2000 when we started completing placements with local clients in South Florida that needed computer programmers, we fulfilled our first dream and leased a brand-new Lexus LS400. We were proud to be the first owners of a foreign car in our families. And this was not just an ordinary foreign car; it was an automobile of beauty. With the blessing of our CPA, knowing we would use the car routinely to visit clients up and down I-95 as well as meeting every newly hired programmer for lunch ahead of their start date, we were able to use company profits to make the monthly payment. Although this expense would have been an addback at the time of a divestiture, it was an example of a **_lifestyle decision_** with company funds.

An alternative course of action would have been to never use any of the company's profits except to grow the company. Although the car payment at that time was $1,000 a month, that money could have been better utilized for other opportunities. Before starting a company or even after you have started your company you have to decide on a path and ideally that should happen as soon as possible.

Our *lifestyle* company provided us with many benefits. We were able to hire our children first in part-time roles while they were still in school and then as full-time employees after graduation. As owners of the company, we were able to provide health insurance to our family members. At our discretion we took our meetings outside the office and had lunches and dinners at restaurants we normally would have dined at only once or twice a year. We were very generous over the years to bring in meals to our staff, which was a motivational tool. We could, however, have limited it to special occasions.

Our biggest and perhaps most magnificent spending was on company cruises and holiday parties. The cruises were logistically simple to plan because we were based in Coral Springs, less than an hour from Port Everglades. Again, the cruises were motivational in nature and were tied to goals, but they were not fiscally responsible decisions. We could have easily replaced those events over the years with less expensive team-building activities. And our holiday parties as well were usually without budgets. We partied at most of the nicer hotels and restaurants with the entire team.

We never hired a CFO. Every time Mike contemplated that he was irritated by the salary requirements candidates asked for. As a result, Mike counted on the experience of his controller Cody. A CFO would have a stopgap ahead of the spending that Mike and Patty approved. A CFO is a must-have in a company that has intentions to grow fast and sell fast. If we had to do it all over again, we would have chosen a similar path, perhaps mixing *lifestyle* management with more recognized and acceptable accounting practices.

VI. A CASE STUDY: DR. KRIS

As with most of the stories presented in this book, this anecdote is true, but we have changed names for obvious reasons. Dr. Kris was a well-known, well-respected, and well-liked primary care doctor working for a large hospital system in the state of Florida. As has occurred in many instances across the country, individual hospitals are bought or merged through acquisition with other individual hospitals and become what we have grown used to—large hospital factories.

This was Dr. Kris's first experience with a large hospital factory. Daily he was expected to see dozens of patients scheduled by his front office and additionally expected not to spend as much time with them as possible. As we all know, time is money. For years, Dr. Kris and his medical assistant, Joy, sprinted through their days, trying to complete as many visits as possible. We were Dr. Kris's patients and in one instance I remember waiting more than an hour to see him. If that wasn't horrible enough, once he came into the room it seemed he was rushing to get on to his next patient. I stopped seeing Dr. Kris after just a few visits.

Over the course of several years, Dr. Kris and Joy were getting frustrated at their requirement to see so many patients daily and, more important, not being able to spend any quality time with their patients. Quality of care simply did not exist.

Dr. Kris had an ambitious spirit. He started thinking about a new model he could employ that would satisfy his burning desire to prioritize quality of care. After long discussions with his family he sat down with Joy and pitched the idea. In an unchoreographed presentation Dr. Kris presented an idea of providing concierge service. The idea had several challenges because he was not able to hire staff just to manage insurance submissions and the follow-up required to collect funds from the insurance companies or his prospective patients. But then he produced the idea of a subscription service. Yes, like Netflix and Amazon he would offer a flat-fee option to new patients billed automatically to their credit cards. There would be no fees for visitation, no copayments, no insurance filings. All the patients would need to do was call, text, or email Joy to make an appointment, then go into the office for a consultation. And the patients could stay as long as they wanted. Joy thought the idea was brilliant. Together they would put in their resignations and open an office, just the two of them, longtime coworkers.

A lot of excitement surrounded the announcement. Local prospects that were once his patients, their friends, their relatives, their parents, and grandchildren would gain access to a new concierge service from a great doctor.

Now, as we described in earlier chapters, first-time entrepreneurs face challenges at a different level. Dr. Kris had one challenge that is not unique to new and existing entrepreneurs, PEOPLE!

Although Joy was excited about the opportunity to continue to collaborate with her old boss, how could he afford to pay her? Joy was working for a publicly traded company, albeit a hospital factory, and was receiving weekly pay and benefits. Dr. Kris could match the weekly pay but was not able to provide benefits just yet, only the promise that he would start a benefits program as soon as the practice was on its feet.

Dr. Kris and Joy had their grand opening, which was preceded by lots of email and work of mouth. Dr. Kris and Joy saw their enrollment grow to 100 patients immediately. And, at a monthly subscription price of only $50, they already had a guaranteed income of $5,000 per month. LIFE WAS GOOD.

At the end of the first year the idea was gaining momentum. The subscription count had grown to 200 and with the new price of $75 per month, the doctor and his medical assistant were grossing $15,000 per month. Joy got a raise!

But as history repeats itself, there were challenges along the way with Joy. On several occasions her car broke down. On another occasion her water heater broke and her apartment flooded. And of course, there were frequent occasions when she must leave early to pick up her son after school. These are all perfectly normal occasions individual business owners must plan for. Dr. Kris, being the good person he is, he helped Joy pay for car repairs, home repairs, and occasional Uber services. He rightfully decided this is what new entrepreneurs should do.

Fast-forward to year two. Dr. Kris and Joy were in the office and could not believe two years had gone by so fast. Their subscription count had continued to grow. Their system of charging a flat monthly fee had taken hold, still no copayments, no insurance claims, no cancellation fees. And Joy had received two more pay increases. But a storm was brewing. Joy had requested Dr. Kris update his computer systems. Although a great idea, it would be prohibitively expensive. Joy also wants a substantial pay raise in addition to a benefits package. And at this point these were not requests; they were demands.

Again, the entrepreneurial doctor was faced with managing an employee challenge he could not afford. Other expenses, including malpractice insurance, were eating away at any profits the doctor's office was making. What should the doctor do? As an entrepreneur, what would you have done?

At a planned meeting several weeks later, Joy advised Dr. Kris she had received an offer from another doctor's office closer to her house. The offer included much higher base pay and benefits. She indicated she was prepared to provide thirty day's notice. Dr. Kris had been preparing for this eventuality. He knew Joy was ready to take the next step in her career, especially with the new experience she had gathered as she sold medical assistance for a highly successful primary care doctor. They shook hands. Dr. Kris's only request was that she remain as professional as she had been until her last day. Often once an employee resigns, regardless of their tenure, their attitudes can change. And that could be especially dangerous when that employee is dealing directly with patients.

A good day, not a great day, ended for the doctor. He reached out to all of his colleagues, posted the opening on multiple job boards, and planned to have a replacement for Joy in the chair before her thirty days were up. But the good day turned bad that night. Joy texted the doctor and said she did not think it was fair the way she had been treated recently. He ignored her many requests. Next, she said that after further consideration, she was not giving thirty days' notice. She was giving one day's notice and she would not be returning.

Dr. Kris was stunned. In his heart and in practice he felt he did everything possible to please his only employee. He never hired a second medical assistant as a potential backup because Joy did not like the idea. (THAT WAS HIS BIGGEST MISTAKE.) He allowed her to work from home, leave early, come in late, manage all the schedules. He did not know what he did wrong. Close to one month later and after a difficult thirty-day period without a medical assistant, Dr. Kris found a replacement.

There is an important lesson in this story. More than one. But the main one is to **PLAN FOR CONTINGENCIES**. How many times have you flown in an airplane with just one engine? Think about why. Dr. Kris started his practice with one engine. And although he thought about the second hire who would have provided redundancy, he never did it.

This is another lesson in **WHAT NOT TO DO** when starting a business. There is, however, a good ending to the story. I visited Dr. Kris. The visit was free because I was now a member of his subscription service, better known in the medical profession as concierge service. In fact, his service is so extraordinary that my wife, married daughter Stephanie, and married son Mike are now also members of his concierge physician practice.

After the usual weigh-in and chatting with his new hire, Dr. Kris was pleased to inform us he had hired a second medical technician for his practice. And this time, May, his replacement hire was overjoyed that she had a backup. This one simple step will not only provide the redundancy necessary in Dr. Kris's practice, but also in all businesses that take the measure to ensure losing one employee can bring down a business.

VII. A CASE STUDY: MS. LOUISE

In 2021 we were finally going to realize our lifelong dream of owning a house that was not in Florida. Since we married, we moved from one city to another within the state, primarily for reasons of employment. In the early 2000s, not long after we started the company, we bought a parcel of land on a mountain top in Asheville, North Carolina. It took more than five years before we were able to complete construction on the property, which had an awesome view of little Pisgah Mountain, part of the Appalachian Mountain chain also known as the Smokey Mountains. We were in love with the area, which is why Stephanie and Anthony ultimately decided on getting married at the Biltmore Estate. Several years after we accepted the occupancy, we fell out of love with the area, mostly because of the heavy traffic, and we sold the house.

Patty immediately started looking for an alternative location. This time, though, she thought we should locate a community that had amenities, maybe one we could get to easily from Florida by auto or by air. And Patty did come through this time in a big way! She found a golf course community that had mountain views again, but this time on the west side of the Smokies. But it was also located directly on the Tennessee River so that we had the best of both worlds, mountains and water. And, if in the future we choose to purchase a horse or two, there is even an equestrian center. After close to two years, we took occupancy of our new lakefront home in August 2023.

Let us introduce Louise, a gentle, kind, and very good-natured entrepreneur who lives and works in Knoxville, Tennessee. We met Louise in 2022 after the house construction was well underway. She was referred by one of the residents in our new community who could not stop bragging about her talent. Like most entrepreneurs, Louise started her career working for someone else. And like most entrepreneurs it did not take long for Louise to realize she would be happier on her own and doing what she liked best on her own timeline. Louise never did do the extensive hiring we did at Ardor; instead she kept her operation limited to just one assistant. As a result, she could never really take on more than one or two projects at a time, which was fine for her.

She had worked with her lead designer, Karolyn, for many years and together with her completed many projects and made very handsome profits. Dealing exclusively with high-net-worth individuals will yield those results. They were a real team. We witnessed it firsthand when they showed up with her new Lexus SUV, which was overloaded with samples of rugs, wallpaper, and patterns for various types of bedding and paints. We were really impressed with their professional approach and hired them for our project.

Approximately halfway through our project, Karolyn dropped a bomb on Louise and quit without notice. We did not know at the time that Louise had been trying to hire a backup, but Karolyn demanded that she did not hire a backup. Was something wrong with this scenario? All Louise was trying to do was build in some redundancy. The story has a very good ending. Louise found someone with more interest and better skills. Together they worked toward completion at our new lake/retirement home. And just recently we referred Louise to the couple who bought the last lake lot in the community. Mark and Tina were equally impressed at the work done in our home and hired Louise almost instantly.

A WORD OR TWO ABOUT REFERRALS

Referrals are priceless and most often great people refer to other great people. Using referrals whether to gain customers or recruit new employees is a tried-and-true method for adding revenue to your top line, and is less expensive than advertising. Over the 20 PLUS years that Patty and I and our leadership team grew the company we probably let go of more than 100 sales people because they could not produce the way that they said they could during the interview process. **_Maybe we should have asked for W2 statements as part of the interview process?_**

It's never too late to update a process, especially one that we believe is working. One of our former leaders made a habit of repeating the phrase, REFERRALS, REFERRALS, REFERRALS at every single sales meeting.

Over the same 20-year period we spent enormous amounts of money on advertising to bolster our internal sales staff. Most years that number exceeded $100,000.00 annually. And, most often those candidates that we agreed to hire did not make the cut and we ended up terminating them. If we added up the lost time and money spent training those candidates our annual spending was likely closer to $200,000.00 per year. Not to mention what negative consequences made their way to the sales floor when we were seen constantly hiring and firing unqualified candidates.

If you are just starting out and preparing to make a hire, I advise that you take the time to hire slowly, and fire fast when necessary. Patiently seek out referrals versus advertising, hiring strangers, and invariably terminating them for lack of production. If you are already building your business and have an existing staff that is working out, ask them for referrals, and pay them fairly for those referrals.

The outcome will yield a happier work environment with like-minded employees, less wasted time interviewing unqualified candidates, and increased profits to the bottom line.

VIII. ON HIRING IN 2025 AND BEYOND

HEADLINE! You do not need very much if any of rental space, especially now with a trend toward remote workforces and an oversupply of all types of rental property.

In 1979, the year Patty and I were married in New York City, we decided to move to Miami, Florida, where Mike's parents lived, and look for work. We were free spirits. Patty would be turning twenty later that year, and Mike would be turning twenty-two a month later. We did not have work. And we had limited skill sets. Looking back, we did not have a care in the world. We picked up a Sunday copy of the *Miami Herald* where the classified advertisement section had pages upon pages of job openings that we felt we qualified for. Fortunately, unlike the first time we looked for work before our marriage, it did not appear that we would have to pay a fee to an agency to find work. This was progress; this was encouraging. Monster.com had not been born yet. This was the best way that we knew of at the time to find work. And the only way unless you were getting assistance from a placement service after graduation.

Fast-forward to 1981. Patty was very happy working for a small family-owned insurance agency. Mike, however, was getting restless and wanted to advance his career with a larger company where he could become a computer programmer full time. And somehow Mike's prayers were answered. An information technology placement firm found Mike and set him up for an interview as a full-time programmer in Fort Myers, Florida. This was the first instance where Mike did not have to scan the newspapers looking for a job. Real progress!

This episode in our lives, however, was more than just another event. It was a big step that gave us the idea to make money helping others find work. The company, Source Services, did all the work – they arranged the interview, arranged to fly us to Fort Myers at the company's expense, and came into our house, packed us, and moved us. Source Services invoiced 30 percent of Mike's base salary for their efforts. Source Services collected $6,000 for their services. Mike and Patty were introduced to staffing at that moment in the spring of 1981.

In the years that followed and as the internet gained momentum, Mike routinely used a growing number of job boards and Source Services to grow his team of professional programmers. Mike was promoted to manager in a few short years and one of his responsibilities was to fill vacant positions.

DICE.COM became another larger marketplace to post open IT jobs along with monster.com. In exchange for a monthly fee paid to dice.com, an employer could post opening IT jobs and have applicants apply directly to those openings. My job as a direct hiring manager job easier as time went on. More programmers started posting their résumés online in search of the highest paying positions available in the areas that they desired.

But as with everything in this short life that we have on Planet Earth, things change. Let me take you into the future. The following will illustrate the processes we now utilize at Ardor Health Solutions to fill our open internal positions.

2024 ACTUAL POSTING

Headline! Ardor Health Solutions is now hiring five healthcare staffing recruiters. Our base salary is $50,000 a year. Do you need extra time off, for family time, for vacation, for anything? As a new member of Ardor Health Solutions, you can expect unlimited paid time off.

The position is based in beautiful Tampa, Florida, one of the most desired cities in the entire state, a state which boasts no state income tax. Your net paycheck will be larger here than in many other states across the United States.

If you are not currently based in Tampa, we can accommodate you, no problem. We have a comprehensive online training program that we offer all new hires for the first three weeks. After you complete your first month of employment, we will fly you into our corporate office for a week of additional in house training and provide you with an opportunity to meet the entire team. As placements of your caregivers are completed you will earn commission, which we pay weekly along with your regular paycheck. If you have a minimum of two years of successful healthcare recruiting experience and have a desire to grow your career with a twenty-year old established family-owned healthcare staffing firm, we encourage you to apply.

The responsibility to seek our new internal hires is a full-time job and requires the commitment of the entire company to be successful. Since our divestiture of our school-based staffing business in October 2020 we have made a commitment to rebuild our sales force. Our chief operating officer, Michael Thomas, has spearheaded this activity. The job posting illustrated above is an example of an actual posting that we had online as of this writing with LinkedIn.com. Because we are advertising *fully remote*, Mike will receive as many as dozens of inquiries weekly. Although the first time Mike posted first advertisement, he received hundreds of résumés in the first two weeks. Mike's first activity requires that he identify candidates that have the minimum requirement of healthcare staffing experience. The more contiguous years of experience at the same employer is very important in the initial selection process. Mike also looks for current employees that are notably recognized competitors of Ardors. Mike will then perform a telephone prescreen, seeking the candidates with the best communication skills. Once the field is narrowed down to ten, Mike will forward the resumes to the leadership team composed of the CEO, president, and operations manager. Without much delay, because if the process takes too long, the candidates will lose interest. The leadership team will set up a series of Microsoft teams meetings with each of the candidates. During these teams meetings, which typically last up to one hour, the team and the applicant get an opportunity to know each other. As a result of these meetings, the applicant pool is typically cut in half. It should be noted that if an applicant misses a scheduled meeting with the leadership team, they are typically removed from the running.

What follows is another Skype with our vice president of human resources and our vice president of operations. On this second one-hour teams call the applicants are provided with all the details of our benefit package and have an opportunity to ask more questions about the company and the position. Although this process appears to be long and tedious, in this new era of hiring we are deciding to bring on new employees that will spend little to no time physically in our home office. Our process concludes with an offer letter that the company and the applicant will countersign using an online program such as DocuSign.

To successfully recruit and hire employees in 2025 and beyond, companies must innovate. By utilizing our model, we can tap qualified candidates from all over the country. The risk is greater because management does not have the physical connection, like when Mike was first job seeking more than thirty years ago. However, because we are employing the latest technology on the laptop computers that we provide upon hire, our managers can monitor telephone time, keystrokes on the laptop, login, and logoff times and more. Our expectation at Ardor Health Solutions is that we will, in the end, make better hires, have reduced turnover, and benefit from increased productivity. Our newest generation in the workforce has asked for the freedom to work remotely. We are prepared to meet that requirement.

IX. MARRIED AND WORKING TOGETHER – THE FINAL CHAPTER

There is an ugly statistic that all couples, including newlyweds and couples already married must deal with in these great United States, more than half of all married couples end up in a divorce. This is particularly true in the 21st century. Our parents were married a little later in life than we were, but the idea of divorce probably never entered their minds. Both our parents were married more than fifty years as it was common for those born into the greatest generation. The men fought in World War II. Then many came home to start families, raise children, and in my father's case, start a business. Patty's dad was trained in automotive sales, found a job, and worked 6 days a week until he retired at sixty-two years old. All four of our parents lived into their early eighties and passed away with dignity.

My mom did collaborate with my dad daily. So, the fact that Patty and I can <u>stay married and work together daily is not surprising</u>, at least to both of us. We did have some key secrets I think that has allowed this relationship, our families, and our business to withstand the ups and downs. We would like to share some of those with you in this last chapter.

ONE At the onset, we had to agree fully exactly what business we were going to start. I believe that if either of us were on the fence about this critical first step our business may have ended up as another statistic, failing very early as 50% of most businesses do. Patty had a passion for people. That was evidenced by the fact that by the time we had started our first business, HighTechGroup, she had raised both Stephanie and MikeT by herself for the most part. Yes, I was home for dinner, but then rushed off to school working on my degree. Once I finished school, I started writing code for local businesses to pay the bills.

I had a passion early on for machines, specifically computers. In 1978 I started attending a technical college and learned my first programming language, BASIC. By the time we started HighTechGroup in 2000, I already had a little over 20 years of programming and management experience, and had my degree. It seemed obvious that we should start a staffing company that employs people on a temporary basis, and that the business would employe computer programmers.

Enough emphasis cannot be placed on how critical this first step is. And, if your decision to go in to a certain does not provide the satisfaction that owning your business must provide, it's OKAY to try a different business. Going back into the workforce after a failed first attempt would be a big mistake in my opinion.

TWO We decided on what business we were going to start, great! But who was going to be responsible and for what? There were only two of us, which meant that our job descriptions were going to be lengthy, and that the last line of our job descriptions would include all other duties as assigned. We both had to agree that there could be no finger pointing and no laziness. Every task must be completed and must be completed well and on time. If one of us became lazy, we have been doomed to failure. In the beginning and continuing to this day, a successful start-up means that there are no short days and no holidays and no weekends. Our recipe was written out and executed with precision. I was on the phone all day collecting requirements for open positions for programmers, computer operators, analysts, network technicians and database administrators. If I collected enough openings early in the day I would switch to calling local candidates and trying to convert them into taking our jobs. Otherwise, I would start making my calls after dinner with the same plans.

During the day Patty was on the internet searching for candidates. We were limited twenty years ago to one single source, Monster.com. But it was a good source and Patty did a good job gathering as many resumes as she could find for me to call that evening. She was also responsible for maintaining communication with the temporary workers that we already had on assignment. Usually that had to do with managing their time and confirming hours.

That's how our work week went in the beginning before we were able to hire more staff. The best days of the week however was Saturday. That's when Patty would get out of bed, before me and go into our home office to begin the billing process. The fax machine starting making noise early on Friday evenings. For us that was our cash register. Every timesheet was copied, one was put in a pile for payroll where Patty then wrote checks on Mondays. The other was placed in a pile for invoicing. And that's what Patty and I most enjoyed. Looking back, it was almost unbelievable when we reached $30,000.00 in billing in a week less than 6 months after we started our first company. We had the responsibility piece of our business working flawlessly.

THREE Now that we are making a profit the next question should be, how do you want to invest that profit? And this question is not meant to be the third recommendation only. This question should be answered frequently and must be agreed upon together. If either of you disagree on how and where to spend your early profits, that will become a problem. This is like being married and having no money which ultimately leads to big fights in a marriage. In my opinion, reviewing this action every quarter, or every other quarter is a good habit to follow. Do you want to hire another resource? In our case do we need more job orders, or do we need another recruiter because we cannot keep up with the open job orders? Do we need a faster computer, fax machine, or do we need to increase the speed of the internet. Is our accounting system up to date? Do we need to find an accountant? The best way to address this issue is to get with your wife, make a list, assign each item on that list a priority, then go for it! Always remember that if you make a mistake, no one will lose their lives. For example, if a doctor makes a mistake in the operating room. Unless you are in the business of repairing humans, mistakes are not costly, and they can always be corrected quickly and without much pain.

FOUR This next paragraph is not meant to offend our readers. Both of have agreed throughout our close to fifty years together on this matter. If at this point in your young company's start-up you have successfully completed sales that have generated a profit, you are winning. Patty and I were very blessed that we were able to convert our idea into a successful start-up in a matter of months. For most, that early success may not come so quickly, particularly depending on what your product or service is, how much it costs, and how many different markets you are serving or planning to serve. Our first start-up focused on the south Florida market exclusively. That decision limited our ability to scale. Our current entity, Ardor Health Solutions, is positioned to do business in all fifty states. If you and your spouse are among the winners, take some time to reflect. That may mean a nice dinner out for the two of you. Surely you both will be discussing business at dinner. You may also want to consider giving thanks, contributing to a charity, or even performing some community service. Personally, we have made a habit of attending a Sunday service every week. And in our case, almost always, we have started our new week refreshed, sometimes with new ideas, and just feeling better about the week ahead. "He who could climb a lofty height must go by steps, not leaps." St. Augustine of Canterbury, Bishop, Italy 605 A.D.

FIVE After 12 months of working together, probably more hours than either of you ever imagined, you may be thinking about hiring extra help. We share two common thoughts here. As my dad said, and stuck to his guns about this. Your wife is your partner. Never hire, although your intentions are honorable, a family member or even a friend. In our history of close to 25 years working together I pushed Patty to hire her brother. He was a hard worker like his dad, and I felt sorry for him. But imagine the family repercussions if we had to fire him because he was not qualified for the job that we hired him for. How would her mom and dad feel if we fired her big brother? What would his wife think, and possibly their children? I am not including your own children in this recommendation. Although that can be tricky, if done properly with generational family intentions in mind, it will work as it has for us.

And, if you both agree that a new hire is necessary, we would suggest strongly that you consider many things including. Like-minded people of the same generation that have quantifiable skill sets, ideally persons that have been referred, and new hires that can generate revenue for your company. We hired our first two employees within the first 12 months of our business. They were both referred by our close neighbors. They both had skill sets that we knew we could use to expand our sales efforts. They both succeeded and we both were pleased that we agreed to hire two people that we both really liked.

SIX There are going to disagreement, which may lead deeper into arguments, which may lead further into outright fights. Every married couple has disagreements about money, raising children, and even eventually taking care of their parents like we had to do. Not surprisingly, owning a business as a married couple has not been much different. The conversations over money when you are successful should be about how to spend it, or invest it. Those conversations for us were the easier ones. And similarly, the conversations about raising children are not much different when it comes to managing employees. We were blessed enough to grow our company to 500 employees at our peak, which was just before we divested our School Division. And there were many conversations that led to disagreements when it came to deciding who stays and who should go. Later in our writing we will go into greater detail regarding the successful ways to developed to manage our staff. **SEE CHAPTER X.**

SEVEN Finally, there were in-depth conversations about when we should divest the company. Over the more than 20-year period that we have run the company there have been multiple occasions when unsolicited buyers approached us with offers in the form of Letters of Intent. In these instances, we were always in unison. It never hurts to listen to what the prospective buyers had to offer. What was very important was that we kept our business private. The last thing that we wanted to happen, VERY IMPORTANT, was to have the staff hear that we were selling the company.

Never go to bed angry at each other. This is a very common phrase that probably should be included in wedding vows. I would be exaggerating the truth if I wrote that over our close to 50 years of marriage and working together, we have never gone to bed angry. But I can write in good faith that our disagreements never went longer than the next morning in the rare cases that it happened. We have always tried to do our best to keep this promise to ourselves. A successful couple must keep this promise.

This morning as we put the finishing touches on our first book in what we hope will become a series of books we are sitting at the kitchen table, working together. Patty just authorized the Met Life bill. I just funded our weekly payroll. We are preparing our eleven o'clock meeting with our new *family leaders* Stephanie and Mike that we now have once a week. We continue to remain committed to our goal of building up the business bigger and better than ever and maybe in the next several years formally passing the business along to our two great children. Stephanie already has two beautiful girls, our Isabella and Adriana. Mike and Samantha, his wife, are entering into the time in their adult lives when they will be having children. Who knows, maybe our grand children will be running the company one day. If it is what God wants.

X. HOW TO STAY CONNECTED

As of this writing Mike and Patty, currently represented in the company as CO-Founders and Board Members, although not actively involved with the day-to-day, are well on their way to growing their company a second time along with the newly formed leadership team that includes our new CEO that was referred to us and our two children Stephanie, now President and Mike T, now Executive Vice President. We also have restructured our Leadership Team to include two highly skilled women that worked for us at Ardor 1.0, and are now respectively Vice President of Operations and Vice President of Human Resources and Benefits. Another piece of the new puzzle came together when our new CEO referred (again REFERRED), his brother-in-law, to head up our new sales team. And the team will grow as it has in the past, without the multiple instances of **BAD DECISIONS** especially when it comes to hiring. Since the end of 2020 when we successfully executed the divestiture of our School Division, we have been experiencing new events on a weekly basis. Those events include constantly analyzing the market place for new opportunities.

We are proud to announce an initiative that will allow the readers of our book an opportunity to stay connected.

---

www.marriedandworkingtogether.com is where you can sign up for our monthly newsletter. You can look forward to a rich source of information, verified, qualified, and quantified with decades of experience, which will help you accelerate the growth of your business, minimize mistakes that we often made, and put your business on a quicker trajectory for a sale event. It is our desire to help you make your financial dreams become a reality. <u>LET'S GROW TOGETHER USING OUR PLAYBOOK.</u>

ABOUT THE AUTHORS

Mike and Patty met one Sunday afternoon in Brooklyn, New York. The event was a twenty-five-year wedding celebration. Mike's godfather from confirmation as it turns out was also Patty's godparents for her confirmation. Is that where the foundation for our long marriage and eventual strong business success started? They had never met before except through a few handwritten letters. Two years later they were married.

Now, close to fifty-years later they have two married children actively running the company and two beautiful grandchildren that they spend a lot of time with. Over the years there have been many ups and downs. However, one thing stayed consistent, they solved every challenge together.

We hope that you enjoy this nonfiction/love story. Mike and Patty.